WRITING
MAGIC

WRITING MAGIC

Creating Stories That Fly

GAIL CARSON LEVINE

Collins

An Imprint of HarperCollinsPublishers

Acknowledgments

Permission is gratefully acknowledged to use the following excerpts:

Page 26: From *Jacob Have I Loved* by Katherine Paterson. Copyright © 1980 by Katherine Paterson. Used by permission of HarperCollins Publishers.

Page 52: From *Lily's Crossing* by Patricia Reilly Giff. Published by Delacorte Books for Young Readers.

Pages 59 and 67: From *The Birthday Room* by Kevin Henkes. Text copyright © 1999 Kevin Henkes. Used by permission of HarperCollins Publishers.

Pages 40–41: Grateful acknowledgment is made to Anne Bernays and Pamela Painter, whose character questionnaire in *What If? Writing Exercises for Fiction Writers* (Addison Wesley Longman) inspired me to develop my own character questionnaire.

Collins is an imprint of HarperCollins Publishers.

Writing Magic

Library of Congress Cataloging-in-Publication Data
Levine, Gail Carson.
  Writing magic : creating stories that fly / Gail Carson Levine.
     p.   cm.
  Publisher-supplied summary: "Newbery Honor author Gail Carson
Levine shares her discoveries for writing exciting stories."
  ISBN-10: 0-06-051960-6 (pbk.) — ISBN-13: 978-0-06-051960-5 (pbk.)
  ISBN-10: 0-06-051961-4 (trade bdg.) — ISBN-13: 978-0-06-051961-2
(trade bdg.)
  1. Fiction—Authorship. I. Title.
PN3355.L397 2006   2006000481
[808.3]—dc 22   CIP
                                                                AC

Typography by Larissa Lawrynenko
❖

To Jack Starkey,
for valor and extraordinary love,
and to the writing kids of Brewster, New York

CONTENTS

Liftoff

CHAPTER 1

✦✱✦

A Running Start

THIS IS A BOOK about writing fiction. But it should help you write anything: e-mails, essays, greeting cards, love letters, skywriting.

Pick one of the options below and use it as the beginning of a story. You can revise the sentences a little or a lot to make them work better for you. Feel free to change the names and to turn boys into girls or vice versa. Write for at least twenty minutes.

Oh, and have fun!

✦ I have one green eye and one brown eye. The green eye sees truth, but the brown eye sees much, much more.

✦ The ghost was eating a peanut butter and jelly sandwich.

✦ "Be nice," my father said. "After all, he's your brother."

✦ I am the most famous twelve-year-old in the United States.

✦ Jason had never felt so foolish before, and he hoped he'd never feel so foolish again.

✦ If somebody didn't do something soon, they were going to have a catastrophe on their hands.

✦ Alison was the runt of the family, born small and ill-favored, and by the time she was thirteen, she was still small and ill-favored.

✦ It was a witchy house: the low-slung roof; that quiet gray paint; those squinting, shuttered windows; and the empty porch rocker that rocked, rocked, rocked day and night.

✦ The first time I saw Stephen, he painted a hex sign on my right arm, and I couldn't move my fingers for three hours.

✦ Ms. Fleming's wig had gone missing.

Okay, you've done it. Congratulations! If you haven't finished your story, save it so you can work more on it later. If you have finished, also save it.

At this point if you want to go back and use one of the other beginnings to write another story, please help yourself. Two stories are better than one, and three are better than two. If you like, you can write ten stories, or double up and write twenty!

Now here are a few rules for this book and for writing:

1. The best way to write better is to write more.

2. The best way to write better is to write more.

3. The best way to write better is to write more.

4. The best way to write more is to write whenever you have five minutes and wherever you find a chair and a pen and paper or your computer.

5. Read! Most likely you don't need this rule. If you enjoy writing, you probably enjoy reading. The payoff for this pleasure is that reading books shows you how to write them.

6. Reread! There's nothing wrong with reading a book you love over and over. When you do, the words get inside you, become part of you, in a way that words in a book you've read only once can't.

7. Save everything you write, even if you don't like it, even if you hate it. Save it for a minimum of fifteen years. I'm serious. At that time, if you want to, you can throw it out, but even then don't discard your writing lightly.

That last rule needs explaining. I used to think, long ago, that when I grew up, I'd remember what it felt like to be a child and that I'd always be able to get back to my child self.

But I can't.

When you become a teenager, you step onto a bridge. You may already be on it. The opposite shore is adulthood. Childhood lies behind. The bridge is made of wood. As you cross, it burns behind you.

If you save what you write, you still won't be able to cross back to childhood. But you'll be able to see yourself in that lost country. You'll be able to wave to yourself across that wide river.

Whether or not you continue to write, you will be glad to have the souvenirs of your earlier self.

The three items below aren't rules; they're vows. Say them aloud.

THE WRITER'S OATH

I promise solemnly:

1. to write as often and as much as I can,
2. to respect my writing self, and
3. to nurture the writing of others.

I accept these responsibilities and shall honor them always.

CHAPTER 2

* * *

Why I Wrote This Book

WHEN I WAS ABLE to make writing my full-time job, I felt like the luckiest person on the planet. So I decided to share my luck and teach a creative writing workshop in my hometown as a volunteer.

I've been doing it for many years now, and it's made me feel more fortunate than ever. I've loved working with the kids who've come to me. I feel privileged to know them.

They're part of the reason for this book. In teaching writing, I've learned more about how I write, more about the way fiction happens, more about the ways my writing gets into trouble and the ways my students' writing gets into trouble. I want to share what I've learned with as many kids as I can.

I write fiction for lots of reasons. One is *power*. I'm in charge when I write. So are you. You create the world of the story. You make the rules.

I write to tell myself a story or to tell it to the child

reader I once was, because I know what she would have liked. I write to change an old story and tell it the way I think it should be told. Most of all, I write to find out about myself. You learn what you're made of when you write. You amaze yourself by making a joke or writing something truly creepy. Huh! you think. I didn't know I could do that.

When I write, I make discoveries about my feelings. This example is a little sad, so get ready.

My father died in 1986, when I was thirty-eight, and my mother died in 1987. In 1989, before any of my work had been published, I wrote a picture book titled *Dave at Night* about an orphan boy who is sent to an orphanage to live. In real life, my father had been an orphan who grew up in an orphanage. In my story the boy has magical dreams about a couple whose son has died, and they have magical dreams about him. The couple and the boy meet when they're awake and fall in love with each other. The couple adopts the boy, and they all live happily ever after.

No one would publish the picture book. I expanded it into a novel, and still no one would publish it. Eventually I put it aside and wrote *Ella Enchanted*. After *Ella* had been accepted for publication, I sent the novel version of *Dave at Night* to my editor.

She rejected it, too, but she asked me to consider revising it. I hadn't looked at it in a few years, so

I reread it—and got a shock.

When I wrote the book, I was still grieving intensely for my parents. I'd thought I was writing about my father the orphan. But when I reread it, I realized the orphan I'd been writing about had been *me*! It was I who missed my parents so much, I wanted a new set.

I was hugely grateful for the insight. Before, I hadn't understood the depth of my feelings, but now I do. And writing got me there.

I was able to rewrite the book, and this time my editor accepted it.

Writing time!

Write a story about a main character who finds a diamond necklace on a seat in his school bus.

That's the idea, but if you need to change it for the story, feel free. If the necklace turns into a hat that enables the wearer to hear people's thoughts, that's okay. If the school bus seat turns into a seat in a movie theater, that's okay, too. Go where your story takes you.

Have fun!

Save what you wrote.

✦ ★ ✦

CHAPTER 3

Shut Up!

WHEN I WAS A KID, I didn't want to be a writer. I wanted to be an actor, or a painter like my big sister. I gave up the acting idea because I thought I was too short to be a star. I kept on painting and drawing, though. I graduated from college and began to work for the New York State government, helping people on welfare find jobs. In my spare time I painted and drew.

But if a painting I began wasn't suitable for framing in the first fifteen minutes—and it rarely was—I'd start hearing chatter in my head that would go something like this: "That's lousy. You don't know what you're doing. You're no kind of painter. You stink."

Obviously this critic in my head was not letting me be a happy painter.

Nowadays when I visit schools, I ask kids if they ever hear that faultfinding chatter while they're trying to do something creative. In every grade lots of hands go up.

When I ask adults, their hands go up, too.

Where does this impossible-to-please chatter come from?

It's born out of and feeds on a certain kind of criticism. Only a certain kind. It doesn't come from the teacher who says that you used a beautiful blue in the lower left corner of your painting, and that if you use the same color in other places, the blue will make the eye move around the page. It doesn't come from the friend who asks you to clarify why your main character yells at his best friend. That kind of criticism is helpful, and you learn from it.

The criticism that sets off the chatter isn't helpful. It attacks. It's not on your side. It belittles you. Somebody tells you you're not smart enough to understand a complicated idea. Somebody else says you have many abilities, but art (or music or math) is not among them. Another somebody announces, "You just don't have a way with words, dear."

For some reason people grab on to such statements. We believe them and let them into our hearts and brains.

When I was little, my father said something pretty wacko. He said, "Women can't sing." Now you and I know that there are legions of wonderful female singers. When my father made the remark, I had records (CDs hadn't been invented yet) with lovely female voices on them.

If I had named some of these singers, my father would

have said, "They're the exceptions that prove the rule."

I don't know what a good answer to that would have been. But I didn't need a good answer for him. I needed a good answer for me.

I believed him. To this day I'm self-conscious about singing. I let a stupid remark rob me of the enjoyment of singing.

Anyway, I kept painting and drawing. Eventually I took a class in writing and illustrating for kids and discovered that I *hated* the illustrating assignments and loved the writing ones. The chatter was quiet when I wrote, letting me like what I came up with.

These days the chatter sometimes starts up while I'm writing, but I can usually make it pipe down. I tell it to let me finish, and then it can say what it wants. By the time I'm done, it's come over to my side, and it's turned helpful.

You can do the same. You can tell that grumbling, griping chatter to *shut up!* It's not an authority. It doesn't know any more than the part of you that's doing the creating.

This is important. Every time you decide one of your ideas is no good or you tell someone that something you wrote is bad—every time you do that, you're letting the chatter win, and you pay a big price. The price is your creativity, which is part of who you are. When you let the chatter win, you hack away at yourself. You stamp down your joy, your freshness, the riches of your nature.

We who continue to be creative—we who battle that chatter—are heroes. Our stories will get written and told, our paintings will be seen, our songs will be heard.

So shut up, chatter!

Writing time!
Do one or both of these exercises:

+ Turn someone you dislike into an animal. It can be a camel or a caterpillar or any kind of animal. Describe the animal. Tell what happens to it in a story.
+ Think of a boy and a girl you know. Picture them as adults. Imagine they are forced to marry each other. Write what their lives would be like. Write their dinner-table conversation on their first anniversary.

Have fun!
Save what you wrote.

* ⋆ *

CHAPTER 4

Eureka!

I AM LIVING PROOF that you don't have to have lots of ideas to be a writer.

I get very few ideas, but when I get one, I don't let it slip away. I write it down, and even if I'm working on something else, I spend a little time thinking about the new idea and writing out my thoughts.

Some of you may get lots of ideas, too many maybe. I wish I had your problem.

But even if you get too many ideas, you can work on only one of them at a time, maybe two at a time. Okay, maybe three. But that's it. The thing is, don't be fickle. Don't abandon a story just because a wonderful new idea knocks on your brain, begging to come in. Write the new guy down and a paragraph or two about it. Then go back to your work in progress.

I don't have a special author way to get ideas. My ideas, I suspect, come from the same places as your ideas: from experiences I've had, from books, from movies, from dreams, from friends, from conversations. Some of your ideas probably come from school assignments. And sometimes your ideas, I bet, seem to pop up out of nowhere. Mine do, too.

I get my best ideas in the shower, because I'm so relaxed there. I also get ideas when I'm doing something repetitive and boring, especially something physical. If I peeled a hundred potatoes, I'm sure I'd have a few ideas by the time I was done, and maybe one would be for what to do with so many naked potatoes!

Relaxation, repetition, and rhythm let the mind fly free.

But what if you think you don't have any ideas at all?

Not to worry.

Just sit in a chair and stay there. Pick up a pen or pencil and a pad, and start writing. Or start tickling your computer keys. That's all. Ideas aren't necessary.

So what do you write?

Well, you can write, "I have no ideas." That's fine. You can write down all the fun things you could be doing if you weren't sitting there writing stupid nonsense. That's fine, too. I've written junk like that many times. Here's a snippet of junk from my notes for my book *Fairest* when I was making myself do some free writing: "This is a stupid exercise. It's painful to type at this pace. My thumb hurts."

Let your mind go, and write what you're thinking. You can write about why you like to write and maybe why you hate it right now. You can write about your best friend's dog and what you think of the color of your eyes.

You see, writing down your meanderings gets something started deep in the recesses of your brain. That distant part of your mind knows that you want to write stories or poems or plays and not endless jabber, and it will get to work. It may take a while. You may have to write this stuff for hours or days or weeks, but eventually that subterranean part of your brain will come through and begin to send you ideas.

Then you have an obligation. You have to work with the ideas your brain sends. You have to use some of them or one of them. That buried, productive, *brilliant* part of you wants to be thanked, and you thank it by using what it sends. If you don't, it will go back to sleep.

You may be able to prime the idea pump. While you're writing junk, you could jot down story possibilities. I've done that. Here are some that I wrote down once when I was having idea trouble:

+ Camp.
+ New school.
+ Escape from bad situation.

+ Unpopular girl in all-girls' school.
+ Kid wants to be something her parents don't want her to be.
+ Overprotective family. Picks child's friends. Child is drawn to kids not picked. Child feels obligation to parents. Feels the pain of their lives. Stratagems so parents don't know.
+ Fictional book about Jane Austen, which would be a lot about writing.

By the way, if you like any of these ideas, use them.

You could write a list of the kinds of stories you like to read. You could write a sentence or two about your favorite book. You could write about the possibility of writing a similar tale and what that tale might be.

Or you could write down qualities of people, such as mean, friendly, gossipy, generous. Then you could write about how you might use these qualities to create characters.

If you write this sort of thing, you can even graduate your writing. You can stop thinking of it as junk and start calling it notes.

But junk works, too, and I need to write junk. I write plenty of notes, but I've never stopped writing junk.

+ + + + +

Writing time!

Let's try what I've just said. Write down twelve new story ideas right now. Don't expect them all to be good. What you want are twelve ideas, good, bad, or blue with pink stripes. If twelve don't arrive immediately, write junk or notes till you're done.

Have fun!

Save what you wrote.

CHAPTER 5

Getting into It

WHEN YOU START writing a story, all the beginning needs to do is get *you* into the story—only you and nobody else. It's too early to worry about drawing the reader in. At this point it's a waste of time to keep rewriting the beginning to make it better. If something marvelous pops out, that's nice. But if it doesn't, it doesn't matter. When you finish the story and go back to revise it, your beginning is likely to change.

Even if you've figured out your whole story in advance, and you know everything that will happen, your beginning still may change. By the time you've completed the first draft, you'll have an idea of what's important and exciting to open with.

I often start by writing information that I have to know but the reader doesn't. I don't realize this while I'm doing it. Here's an example from my first draft of *The Fairy's Return*:

When Robin was fifteen his family began to believe that he had become a simpleton. If they had known the truth they would have been certain he'd become a complete idiot.

The truth was that—although a baker's son had no business doing such a thing—he'd fallen in love with Princess Lark, heiress apparent to the kingdom of Biddle. Robin wasn't even heir apparent to the bakery. That honor belonged to his oldest brother Nat. And Robin wouldn't ever be baker's first assistant either. Robin's next older brother Matt would hold that position. Someday Robin would be baker's second assistant, which was hardly a title at all.

These paragraphs don't appear in the final book, but I had to write them, and then I was able to discard them. Here's the final, much-revised beginning of *The Fairy's Return*:

Once upon a time in the kingdom of Biddle a baker's son and a princess fell in love. This is how it came about—

Robin, the baker's son, rode to Biddle Castle in the back of the bakery cart. His older brothers, Nat and Matt, sat on the driver's bench with their father, Jake, who was a poet as well as a baker.

I don't plan out my books ahead of time, so sometimes the story I start isn't the story I wind up with, isn't even a distant cousin. When that happens, my original beginning gets escorted out and transferred to different territory in my computer.

If beginnings terrify you, or if you just plain don't like writing them, or if they bore you, skip 'em. Suppose you're writing a tale about a girl who's in a bank when a robbery takes place. Suppose the part that interests you is the robbery itself, but you think that you have to tell the reader who the girl is and why she's in the bank on that fateful day. So you start writing that she's fifteen years old and she's spending the day with her cousin and her cousin's mom. They're going to see a movie, but first the mom has to stop at the bank. You're writing this, and it seems dull, and you can hardly keep writing because you're falling asleep. What should you do?

Bag it! Go right to the robbery, and tell yourself you'll see later what the reader needs to know about your main character and her relatives. It could even turn out that the robbery *is* the right beginning, and that the background info will fall into place naturally or will be unnecessary.

On the other hand, you may feel more comfortable starting with the girl and her cousin and her cousin's mom. You may want to get to know everybody before the robbery.

That's okay, too. Start where you need to, with what appeals to you, what keeps you writing.

And don't worry about beginnings.

Writing time!

Begin a story at three different points. The story will be about a competition. It can be a footrace, boat race, space-ship race, or it could be a chess match, a storytelling contest, an audition for a play. Any kind of competition is fine.

For the first starting point, open your story with the moment the competition begins. Write a page, and then stop.

For the second starting point, go further back in time, and open with the moment the main character finds out that there's going to be a competition. Write a page, and then stop.

For the third starting point, open with the moment the main character begins to prepare for the competition. Write a page, and then stop.

Which beginning makes you the most eager to write the story? Why?

Keep going with that beginning.

Have fun!

Save what you wrote.

CHAPTER 6

✦ ✦

Noticing

ONCE EVERY HOUR tomorrow pay special attention to your senses.

What do you hear?

Maybe your dog is barking or the television is on. Maybe your teacher is speaking. Listen to his voice. Is it deep and rumbly, or is it a middle tone and clear?

Listen for random noises: a branch knocking into a windowpane, the house settling, the occasional honk of a car horn.

Write down what you hear, even the tiniest, most ordinary sounds. If you can't write them down instantly, because your teacher is handing out midterm exams or because you're brushing your teeth, remember and write them down as soon as you can. And if you are brushing your teeth, write later how that sounds. Don't ignore a sound just because you're making it.

What do you taste?

How does that toothpaste taste? Does it tingle? Do you like it? We taste more than food. We may wake up with terrible tastes in our mouths. If you've ever had a cut in your mouth, you've tasted your own blood. I have a bad habit of chewing on the ends of pencils, so I know the flavor of pencil wood.

You're probably not eating every hour, so notice the tastes of your next meal—and not only the tastes but also the feeling of the food in your mouth: hot, cold, wet, dry, mushy, solid. Eat something you hate. Pay attention to what you don't like about it. Eat something you love. Pay attention to it, too. Write it all down.

What do you smell?

Scents get inside us in ways that sights and sounds can't. Scents can make us remember other times, other places. An odor can make us choke or sneeze or even run out of a room. I'll never forget the smell of pond scum on our dog Jake after he went swimming. More pleasantly, the scent of a pie, more than the sight of one, can make us hungry.

Do you smell anything?

You may not. Humans don't have a very strong sense of smell. If you don't smell anything during the first hour, keep trying. Maybe next time you'll catch a whiff of garlic on someone's breath, or a woman nearby will be wearing perfume. Or, if you live in the country as I do, you'll smell a skunk. Write it down.

What do you feel?

Wherever you are, touch something. Touch your blue jeans or something else you're wearing. Is the cloth soft or stiff? If you're at your desk, touch the desktop. Is it warm or cool? If it's made of wood, is the wood smooth or grainy? If it's your desk at school and it's like my desks when I went to school, something's been carved into the wood. Trace the carving. Go to a sink and run your hand under the tap. It's hard to describe what water feels like, but see what you can do. Try writing a poem about the feel of water.

What do you see?

Are you somewhere brightly lit? Or so dark you can barely see? Is the light yellow in tone, or is it white? Pay attention to colors and shapes.

Does what you're seeing have an emotional effect on you? For example, seeing a stain on my favorite T-shirt would annoy me, but seeing a friend's face can make me happy.

If you're in a familiar place, see if you can spot something you never noticed before. Then see if you can spot a second new thing. Write them down.

Humans may not be great smellers, but we are great see-ers, so you should have lots to write about what you see.

Okay, you've done it. You've recorded a day's worth of

sensations. Here's why I wanted you to do it: When you tell readers what your characters are hearing, tasting, smelling, touching, and seeing, then your readers will experience it all, too, and they'll be drawn into your story.

This passage is from *Jacob Have I Loved* by Katherine Paterson. It puts me right there in the marsh in the body of Sara Louise Bradshaw:

> *As a child I secretly welcomed the first warm day of spring by yanking off my shoes and standing waist deep in the cordgrass to feel the cool mud squish up between my toes. I chose the spot with care, for cordgrass alone is rough enough to rip the skin, and ours often concealed a bit of curling tin or shards of glass or crockery or jagged shells not yet worn smooth by the tides. In my nostrils, the faint hay smell of the grass mingled with that of the brackish water of the Bay, while the spring wind chilled the tips of my ears and raised goosebumps along my arms.*

Writing time!

Use the point of view of a young puppy or kitten who somehow, miraculously, is able to think in English. The puppy or kitten is new to seeing, hearing, smelling, tasting, and touching. He doesn't know what anything is, what anything means. He's in the same room you're in right now. His mother and his littermates can be there, too, if you like. Describe what his eyes, ears, nose, tongue, and paws tell him. Does he understand everything, or does he misunderstand some things?

After you've described his first moments, imagine what happens next. Turn it into a story. Remember to put in sensory information as you go along.

Have fun!

Save what you wrote.

Heart and Guts

CHAPTER 7

* ⋆ *

The Nitty-gritty

DETAILS LIGHT UP your fictional world.

Imagine going to your kitchen for a glass of water. Right now. Picture it.

Where are the glasses kept? The answer is a detail. Do you have to stand on something to reach them? What is it? The answer is a detail. What are the glasses like? What color? Are they glass, paper, or plastic? If they're glass, are they heavy? (If you're not sure of the answers to any of these questions, go and check them out.) The answers are details. Turn on the tap. How long do you have to wait for the water to get cold? You guessed it. The answer is a detail. When you turn off the tap, does the faucet drip for a while? Another detail.

Remember the noticing you did in the last chapter. Use your senses. Does the stream of water feel hard because there's a lot of water pressure? Or does it feel soft because there isn't much? How does the water sound? What do you see above the sink? What do you see in the sink? Is the inside of the sink metal or enamel? Are the faucets chrome, and is the chrome shiny?

Some details are sensory. Some are not. What kind of shoes are you wearing right now? The answer is a detail. Are the shoes new, or are they worn out? If you're wearing socks, what color are they? Enough with your feet—what are you wearing on the rest of you? T-shirt and shorts? Or are you dressed up for your brother's high school graduation? What do you like most about the way you look? What do you like least? The answers are all details.

I'm sitting at my computer right now. I have wrist braces on both hands, because typing has given me carpal tunnel syndrome. I'm wearing a wedding ring on my left hand and, on my right, a ring my parents gave me for my eleventh birthday. I'm a tiny person. I haven't grown much since that birthday, and the ring still fits—sort of. Over the years my middle finger and my pinky gradually pressed the ring from a circle into an oval, and I can no longer take it off. It's gold, with side-by-side hearts, one right side up, the other upside down. On the left-hand heart the letter *G* is engraved. On the right-hand heart the letter *C* is engraved. The letters are in script, and the way the *C* is written, it could also be an *L*. That pleases me, since I'm a Carson and a Levine now.

These all are details.

Writing time!

Your main character is participating in a scientific investigation of a magical object. She has a microphone, and all kinds of monitors (heart, lungs, skin temperature, brain function, and anything else you like) are attached to her. A team of scientists is present. She is led to a table where she finds four magical objects:

+ A ring that makes the wearer invisible.
+ A hearing aid that enables the wearer to hear anything on earth, no matter how distant.
+ A magical cookie. Whoever eats it grows taller at the rate of a foot per minute.
+ A magical drink. Whoever drinks it shrinks at the rate of three inches per minute.

Your character must choose an object and wear it or eat it or drink it. Then she must speak into the microphone and tell the scientists everything that happens, without skipping a single detail, no matter how minor. For example, if she's putting on the ring, does the effect start as soon as she touches it or only when the ring is all the way on? So she might report like this: "It's too big for my ring finger. I'm putting it on my index finger. It's over my nail. I don't feel anything yet." Don't leave anything out.

If you like, when she finishes talking to the scientists, she can have an adventure with the object.

Have fun!

Save what you wrote.

* ★ *

CHAPTER 8

The Kiss of Life

THE DETAILS ABOUT getting a drink of water in the last chapter aren't particularly interesting—not by themselves, anyway. But suppose we're reading a story about a woman named Serena, and suppose in the course of the story we grow to like and care about her.

Then she catches pneumonia. She's running a high fever. She's weak and dizzy. She has nurses around the clock, but the night nurse tends to fall asleep and is almost impossible to waken.

Serena wakes up at three o'clock in the morning desperately thirsty. She reaches for the water pitcher next to her bed and knocks it over, spilling out the water. She calls for the nurse, but the nurse doesn't come. She decides to get water herself, even though her doctor has told her to stay in bed, even though she could die if she falls.

Some of the details about getting a glass of water have become interesting now, haven't they? We feel Serena's thirst. When she runs her hand under the tap, that ordinary act comes alive. We're right there, feeling the water. And if she has to climb on something to reach a glass, we're frightened for her.

Here's another example. Billy is starting a new school, and he's heard that the teachers there are very strict. He goes off to school, and the author of Billy's story writes, "By the end of the day Billy knew that the teachers were mean and strict."

That doesn't tell us much, does it? *Mean* and *strict* are generalizations. Nothing detailed about them. And because of the lack of detail, we don't get involved in the story.

Suppose the author does include details, but the wrong ones. Suppose he writes about the number of kids in each class, the color of the walls in the hallways, the kinds of desks in the classrooms, and the food selections in the cafeteria.

We're still not involved in the story.

But suppose the author writes, "In homeroom the girl next to Billy hummed softly while Mr. Paynestrom took attendance. Mr. Paynestrom heard her and slammed his attendance book down on her desk. He stuck his face right up to hers and yelled for five whole minutes. Wow! Billy thought. The teachers here really are mean and strict!"

Now we start caring. There are details, and the right ones, too. My favorite is Mr. Paynestrom's menacing nearness to the girl's face. I can imagine them both, even though

I haven't been told what they look like.

So what makes a detail the right detail?

The right details plunk us down inside a story and put us in our characters' shoes. If we're at a tense point in a story, they heighten the tension. The details tell us that in Billy's school just humming can set a teacher off. So we start to worry about Billy. What if he drops his pencil at the wrong moment? With Serena the details make us feel her desperate thirst. They make us fear that she'll fail to get the water or that she'll hurt herself.

Details can also create an atmosphere. The passage below is from *Dave at Night*. Dave's father died the week before, and his stepmother has brought him to an orphanage. This is how the Hebrew Home for Boys appears to Dave when he sees it for the first time:

> We turned the corner, and I saw the front of the asylum. My eyes traveled up to where a pointy tower rose, like a witch's hat, three stories above the entrance. Below the tower was a clock, and on each side of the clock was a smaller pointy tower. The whole building was only four stories high in the highest part, the middle section. The rest was just three, but each story was very tall. The building wasn't made for people. It was made for witches, with plenty of room for their hats.

The pointy towers and the witches' hats aren't inviting, are they? It's not a building I'd want to walk into, let alone call home.

Now it's your turn.

Writing time!
Pick either or both of these:

✦ Ken is mad at his mother, and he's running away from home. Write a story about how he does it and what happens, using details to heighten the tension. Some opportunities for tension may be: sneaking out without getting caught, walking along a dark road at night, meeting a stranger.

✦ Four kids are invited to their teacher Ms. Frist's house for lunch. Write a story about the lunch, using details to create atmosphere and to reveal the teacher's character. Is the house cozy and welcoming, or is it weird, or is it something else entirely? What does Ms. Frist serve for lunch? Does she have kids of her own? Pets? A husband? What are they like?

Have fun!
Save what you wrote.

⋆

CHAPTER 9

Character Helper

Astory's plot is mostly determined by character. Think about Cinderella. In the original fairy tale she's sweet and kind. But suppose she's a grouch and won't do anything for anybody. How does the story change?

Or suppose she's incompetent. She wants to help her stepsisters dress for the ball, but she rips their gowns by accident. She burns the older sister's hair with a curling iron, and she uses the wrong color shoe polish on the younger sister's dancing slippers. What happens to the story then?

It changes, doesn't it? Maybe she goes to the ball and steps on the prince's toes so many times, he stops dancing with her. But that would depend on the prince's character, too. He could be sick of perfection and might enjoy Cinderella's ineptness.

In real life everyone does things a little differently. If three people are given gift-wrapped boxes for their birthday, each will respond uniquely, and their responses will shed light on their characters. One person may cut the ribbon and tear off the wrapping paper. Another may work at the knot in the ribbon and then ease off the Scotch tape and fold the wrapping paper carefully before opening the box. The third may hug the giver and put the gift aside to open later.

Pay attention the next few times you give people gifts. Observe yourself when your birthday comes around.

Everybody goes about getting dressed differently. Your older brother may try on each of his T-shirts before putting on the same one he wore yesterday, and your little sister may happily put on the shirt your mother picked out.

Everybody even has a slightly different way of brushing teeth and combing hair. And so on.

Below is a neat tool for developing your characters, a character questionnaire. When you use it, don't limit yourself to the space provided here. Expand as much as you need to.

Name: _____

Nickname, if any: _____

Kind of being (human, animal, extraterrestrial, fantasy or fairy-tale creature): _____

Age: _____

Sex: _____

Appearance: _____

Occupation, if applicable: _____

Family members: _____

Pets: _____

Best friend: _____

Describe his/her room: _____

Way of speaking: _____

Physical characteristics (posture, gestures, attitude):

_____

Items in his/her pockets or backpack or purse: _____

Hobbies: _____

Favorite sports: _____

Talents, abilities, or powers: _____

Relationships (how s/he is with other people): _____

Fears: _____

Faults: _____

Good points: _____

What s/he wants more than anything else: _____

For example, under "Way of speaking," your character may always speak a little too loudly, perhaps because her father is hard of hearing. Or under "Physical characteristics," your character might check out his appearance whenever he passes a mirror or even a darkened window in which he can see his reflection. Or under "Relationships," your character might give in easily to the demands of her friends because she hates to argue

Before I begin a new book, I may fill out character questionnaires for some of the main characters. I did one for Char when I was writing *Ella Enchanted*. I don't always complete every item, only those that apply to my story.

However, I'm more likely to use the character questionnaire after I've begun my book. There may be a character I don't understand, and I fill out a questionnaire to gain insight into him.

When I was writing *The Two Princesses of Bamarre*, I couldn't figure out King Lionel, the princesses' father. I knew he had to be cold and useless, but I wasn't sure in what way. The answer came when I got to the "Items in his pockets" question. When I peeked into a pocket, I found *The Book of Homely Truths*, a book of stupid sayings that seem profound, like "Thought must follow action as well as precede it." Or "The impetuous man is overtaken by his desires." And "Poverty means more to the poor than to the rich. Wealth means more to the rich than to the poor."

King Lionel consults the book constantly and uses it as a barrier to genuine connection with people. For example, if you were Lionel's daughter and you went to him, weeping because your cat had just died, he wouldn't hug you. He wouldn't cry either, even though the cat also belonged to him. No. He'd pull out *The Book of Homely Truths* and read you a saying.

Once I discovered *Homely Truths*, King Lionel was a snap to write, and fun, too.

Here are excerpts from character questionnaires for the fifth in the Princess Tales series, *For Biddle's Sake*. The first excerpt is a description of the fairy Bombina's appearance:

> *Large, red-faced, wild black hair, meaty hands, often sweaty, big brown eyes, broad grin, fleshy pink wings, flickering rainbow of lights, small ears (rarely seen, but the same shape as her wings)*

The second is a description of King Humphrey IV's way of speaking:

> *Tends to shout, and pitch rises when he does. His voice is more air than voice.*

Very little from these descriptions went into the book. Still, the information was important for me to know.

Now suppose you've filled out the character questionnaire for your main character. She's an empress, and you've written that she can read minds. You start your story and write in a plot to overthrow her. Several people know about it, but the empress can't know. So her mind reading no longer fits the story. Just change it, and delete any earlier mentions of her special power.

You can change your characters. Just because something's on the character questionnaire doesn't mean you're stuck with it.

Writing time!

Bring a pad with you the next time you're going to be with strangers, such as in a restaurant, in a store, or on a bus. Pick one of the strangers. Observe him carefully. Jot down some notes on his appearance, manner, smell (if you can detect it), and way of speaking. If you're in a situation where you can't jot anything down, then memorize him, and write your notes the first second you can. When you get home, complete a character questionnaire about him. You'll have to invent a lot, so go ahead, but make your inventions fit your observations. For example, if he needs a shave and one of his shoelaces is untied, you might guess that his home is messy.

Repeat with two other strangers. Now put the three of them in a story together.

Here's another exercise: Invent three characters. Write a page for each one, describing how he or she wakes up and does his or her early-morning routines, preparing for work, school, or camp. Put them in a story together.

Have fun!

Save what you wrote.

CHAPTER 10

Suffer!

W HY DO YOU KEEP reading a book?

Usually to find out what happens.

Why do you give up on a book and stop reading it?

There may be lots of reasons. But often the answer is you don't care what happens.

So what makes the difference between caring and not caring?

The author's cruelty.

And the reader's sympathy.

We keep turning pages because we're worried. Horrible things are happening to the heroine (some of which she may be causing), and we have to find out if she comes through them all right. The horrible things can be funny horrible or serious horrible. The head of her Halloween lion suit can get stuck on backward. Or her best friend can die.

There was an old ad for Perdue chickens that said, "It takes a tough man to make a tender chicken." Well, it takes a mean author to write a good story.

The problem is, sometimes we don't want bad things to happen to our main character because we like her. We don't want Cinderella's stepsisters to be too awful, because we identify with Cinderella so much. She's our main character, and we see the story through her eyes. In a way we *are* Cinderella, and we don't want terrible things to happen to us.

Stifle those kind feelings! Have Cinderella burn herself cooking her stepfamily's breakfast. Make one of the stepsisters slap her. Let the family dog bite her.

And watch your reader turn pages, stay up late to finish, get in trouble at school for reading your story in his lap.

I don't mean that your story has to lurch from disaster to disaster. There may be quiet interludes while you set up the action or introduce a character or two. You can give Cinderella a break occasionally, usually between two truly horrible events. But not many breaks, and don't let them last very long.

For example, in *Ella Enchanted* I give Ella a five-page rest with the elves after she's run away from finishing school and before she gets captured by ogres.

But even while Ella is resting, the reader knows that she's still cursed with obedience. Here's a rule: Your hero should never solve all his problems at any point in your story before the end. He can solve one problem, but another one must still be looming.

So be cruel. Make your hero suffer!

Be doubly cruel. Make your reader like your heroine, so the reader suffers when she does. If Little Red Riding Hood tortures and kills a nestful of baby birds on her way to Grandma's house, we're not going to like her a lot, and we're probably not going to mind much when the wolf eats her. We're going to stop caring about Grandma, too, if we discover that her cottage is made of gingerbread and she likes to cook and eat little girls who aren't her granddaughter.

Our main character doesn't have to be a paragon of virtue in order for us to care about him, in order for him to be sympathetic. He'd probably be boring if he were perfect. He can have lots of faults. He can drive us crazy with the jerky things he does.

But he can't be evil. He has to mean well underneath it all.

He also has to be vulnerable. If he's a superhero and nothing can harm him, we're not going to worry about him. There has to be at least one way he can be hurt. Even Superman is in danger from kryptonite.

You want to give your main character a problem that the reader will identify with. In *Ella Enchanted* Ella's problem is that she has to do whatever she's told. We all—even the queen of England—sometimes have to do things we don't want to. And to *always* have to do what we're told would be horrible. We're worried already.

Intensify your brutality. Make sure that we, your readers, know exactly how much your hero is suffering. Plunge us into his mind and heart. Tell us what Robin Hood is thinking and feeling when dire things are happening—and even when dire things aren't happening. When we read the hero's thoughts and feelings, we are lifted out of ourselves and plunked down inside his skin. We breathe with him. We sigh with him. We see through his eyes, hear through his ears, think his thoughts, feel his emotions. We are *in* the story, exactly where you want us to be. No way we're going to stop reading then.

Writing time!

You're going to make your character go through just about the worst thing that can happen to someone. Whether you yourself are a boy or a girl, write from Little Red Riding Hood's point of view what it feels like to be eaten by the wolf. Be sure to tell us what she's thinking when she sees those pointy fangs, when the wolf takes his first bite. Tell us what she sees and hears and smells. Take us there.

I know of two versions of "Little Red Riding Hood." In

one a hunter kills the wolf and slits open his stomach, and Grandma and Little Red Riding Hood step out unscathed. In the other version, Grandma and Little Red Riding Hood get eaten. Period. That's the end of the story. There's no rescue.

For this exercise, you can use either version, although I hope you choose the second one. If you do, and if you write it in the first person, Little Red Riding Hood will be dead at the end, so you're going to need to have her narrate as a ghost or from an afterlife.

If you choose the version with the hunter, be sure to make her thoroughly miserable while she's being ingested, even though she does survive.

So make Little Red Riding Hood *suffer*, and have fun doing it!

Save what you wrote.

CHAPTER 11

* * *

Talking

DIALOGUE LOOKS lovely on the page.

If there's just narrative, the paragraphs are usually longer than dialogue paragraphs. Most readers (idiots or geniuses) get discouraged when they see only three or four long paragraphs on a page. We may not be aware of it, but deep down we're thinking: It's going to be hard to get through this.

But when we see dialogue—short paragraphs, lots of white space—we think: Ah. I can handle that. That looks like fun.

On the other hand, you shouldn't have just dialogue in a story. You need narrative to move characters from place to place, to allow time to pass, to let the reader see the action unfold.

As you write dialogue, think about the white space on the page, and don't let your characters speak in long paragraphs. If a character has a lot to say, break it up. Let whoever she's talking to chime in with a question. Or stop the speech while the other character makes a physical gesture. Or interrupt the speech for a minor event: a stiff breeze, a noise on the stairs, the sun breaking through the clouds. It's best, naturally, if these gestures or events connect with the story.

Below is an example of what I mean, from *Lily's Crossing* by Patricia Reilly Giff.

> *"I have to tell you . . ." Poppy's eyes were open now, blue with paler flecks of gray, his face suddenly serious.*
>
> *"The Dillons left for Detroit," she said quickly. "Mr. Dillon's going to be a foreman in a factory in charge of making planes. Top secret, Margaret says."*
>
> *Poppy grinned. "It won't be top secret for long, not if Margaret knows about it."*
>
> *Lily swallowed, watching him smile.*
>
> *He reached out, put his hand on the oars. "I have to go too. I came tonight to tell you."*
>
> *She didn't look at him. "To a factory like the Dillons? When would we leave?"*
>
> *She looked out across the water, seeing him shake his head from the corner of her eye.*
>
> *"The army needs engineers," Poppy said.*

Short bursts of speech seem natural to the reader. In real-life conversation, people sometimes do speak at length and without interruption. But when we're reading, long speeches usually seem awkward and stiff.

In the selection on the opposite page, the author starts a new paragraph whenever the other character speaks or does something. When Lily swallows, she gets her own paragraph. The separate paragraphs make everything crystal clear.

Just as long speech paragraphs seem unnatural, so do long speech sentences. And so do long words.

Suppose a girl named Abigail is telling her cousin Brynn about a fire that broke out at school. Does this dialogue seem natural to you?

> "My first suspicion of trouble came during language arts when my nose detected a whiff of smoke," Abigail said.
>
> "That whiff must have frightened you. Did you realize immediately that the cause was a fire?"
>
> "Not immediately. Our classroom is located near the science laboratory, and so initially I thought that the smoke originated there."
>
> "Since I've had similar experiences, I would have agreed with you. What caused you to revise your opinion?"

"I changed my mind when our principal, Ms. Montolio, began to address us over the PA system. I didn't think she'd trouble us simply because of a chemistry experiment."

Sounds funny, doesn't it? Maybe a reporter and an arson investigator on TV would sound this way, but not two kids. How about this:

"I smelled smoke in language arts," Abigail said. *"Not much. Just a whiff."*

"That must have been scary. Did you know right away it was a fire?"

"Uh-uh. Language arts is next door to the science lab. There are weird smells all the time."

"Tell me about it. When did you realize what was going on?"

"Well, Ms. Montolio's our principal. I knew something was wrong when her voice came out of the PA system. She wouldn't do that over a science experiment."

See? The second version sounds true to life, doesn't it? More the way people really talk.

My computer did an analysis of each version. Here's how they stack up:

FIRST VERSION

102 words

9 sentences

11 words in an average sentence

19 words in the longest sentence

5 letters in an average word

SECOND VERSION

84 words

13 sentences

6 words in an average sentence

14 words in the longest sentence

4 letters in an average word

So in the second version, the words were shorter, and there were fewer of them. The sentences were shorter, too, but there were more of them.

Writing time!

Pick one or more of these, and write the dialogue:

+ Kelsey wants to borrow a sweater from her older sister, Nadia. Nadia doesn't want to lend it to her.
+ Ian accuses his friend Richard of not playing fair (they can be playing any kind of game or sport).

Richard denies the accusation.

+ Janelle tells a secret to her best friend, Shannon. Shannon doesn't believe her.

+ Meredith explains to her teacher Mr. Ronson why she didn't turn in a book report.

Remember to keep your words and sentences short. Break up the speeches with the other person's questions, gestures, or thoughts. Start a new paragraph whenever the next person speaks, does something, or thinks.

Have fun!

Save what you wrote. In this case, save it in a special place, because we'll be going back to this exercise later.

CHAPTER 12

* ⋆ ✦

Back to Beginnings

IN CHAPTER 5, "Getting into It," I said you don't have to worry about writing a good beginning when you start a story. But you do have to deal with it eventually.

Eventually has arrived.

Which of these beginnings do you think is better?

> *The bear charged.*

Or:

> *It was a lovely morning. The air was mild. Tulips dotted the field with their lollipop colors. A woodpecker tapped out the rhythm of spring, and a lark sang the melody.*

I think "The bear charged" is better. It's got action. It's exciting. Readers are already beginning to worry, even though they don't yet know who's in danger.

The descriptive beginning is pretty but static. The only action comes from the woodpecker and the lark.

I can think of a way to turn the descriptive paragraph into a decent beginning. Suppose a spaceship is about to land and transform that perfect landscape into a crater twenty miles across. Then the static beginning would be important, because the reader would contrast the beauty with the devastation that follows.

We can ratchet up the excitement even more. Suppose we add one initial sentence so that the beginning reads:

> *The fortune-tellers issued their warnings and left the countryside.*
>
> *It was a lovely morning. The air was mild. Tulips dotted the field with their lollipop colors. A woodpecker tapped out the rhythm of spring, and a lark sang the melody.*

What do you think? I think the reader is interested now, a little worried. She wants to know more, so she keeps reading.

Pull five of your favorite books off your shelves. Read the first page or so of each. Look for the ways the author hooks you on the story.

Here are beginnings I can't resist from five books on my shelves:

"I have a zoo in my room." From A Room with a Zoo *by Jules Feiffer*

A zoo? With tigers? I can't put it down.

"It was the nothingness that woke her up." From Blood Secret *by Kathryn Lasky*

Nothingness makes this beginning. *Nothingness* is too interesting to abandon.

"Two of the things Benjamin Hunter received for his twelfth birthday took him completely by surprise: a room and a letter." From The Birthday Room *by Kevin Henkes*

I'm just as surprised as Benjamin. Nobody ever gave me a room. And what does the letter say?

"I've never told this to anyone before, at least not all of it." From Dangerous Skies *by Suzanne Fisher Staples*

Who can resist a secret?

"Two old white ladies came to our village late one day, just before dinnertime, at the beginning of the dry season." From Go and Come Back *by Joan Abelove.*

I want to know who's talking. The narrator pulls me in, and I can't break free.

You can start with action, with mystery, with atmosphere, with a character, with surprise.

Writing time!

Take out one of your stories, even if it's not finished. Read it over. Did you start it in the right spot? Or do you see a place farther along that would be better? If you have to cut vital information to start there, can you fill the reader in later?

If you don't find a beginning that pleases you, you can add one. Write a list of the possibilities.

Of course, your original beginning may be fabulous. If it is, don't touch it.

When you've finished with that story, take out two more, and do the same thing with their beginnings.

Have fun!

Save your revisions.

CHAPTER 13

* ⋆ *

Where Am I?

WHEN I WROTE *Ella Enchanted*, I brought magic and magical creatures into the story right away with the fairy Lucinda and the gift of obedience. The reader knows then that this is fairy-tale land and feels comfortable. If I had waited until page 10 to make something magical happen, the reader would have been surprised. Sometimes you can pull that off, but you have to be careful. More often the reader is confused and may lose confidence in the writer. You don't want that to happen.

The Moorchild by Eloise McGraw begins:

> *It was Old Bess, the Wise Woman of the village, who first suspected that the baby at her daughter's house was a changeling.*

We're clued in already that this is fantasy.

Shabanu: Daughter of the Wind by Suzanne Fisher Staples begins:

> *Phulan and I step gingerly through the prickly gray camel thorn, each of us balancing a red clay pot half filled with water on our heads.*

We're pretty sure we're not in Kansas.

Even in a contemporary story set locally without a shred of fantasy, you still have to establish your world. Your world is different from anyone else's, different even from your best friend's world, although you both are likely to live in the same nation, probably the same town or city. The differences are slight, but they still exist. You have two brothers, and your friend is an only child. You were born in another country and your friend's family has lived in the same house for three generations. You have a secret you've never told anyone. Maybe your friend does, too, but it's an entirely different secret. All these elements make your world unique.

Your characters' world is unique, too.

Wringer by Jerry Spinelli is a contemporary novel about a real custom set in a fictional town. This town raises money to maintain its park by shooting pigeons. You need to reveal a practice like this as early in your story as possible, even though it's true.

Hey, wait a minute! you may be thinking. How can I introduce my character's world when I don't know her world myself yet?

That's okay. Write it the way you think you want it to be. Suppose you're writing a science fiction story. You're in the middle of the story. Your main character, Jeff, has to jump on his atomic sled and deliver medicine to an outpost on the dark side of the planet, where it's always winter. You want things to be as difficult as possible for him, so you make his sled break down. He's trying to fix it when he hears the howl of a dreaded wulff, a distant relative of the wolf on Earth, only wulffs are as big as horses and almost as cunning as humans.

Pretty exciting, right? The only problem is that so far there's been no mention of wulffs. If you bring one in now, your reader is going to smell a rat, not a wulff.

The solution is to go back to the beginning and find a way to drop something in about wulffs. Maybe Jeff's best friend has a wulff scar on his shoulder, and you can show it to us in the first scene.

Writing time!

Imagine a new universe. Think about how it can differ from our own. Describe the inhabitants of the universe, the plant life, and one or more of the following: an eating place, a classroom, a bathroom, a bedroom, a family vacation. Use this universe in a story.

Have fun!

Save what you wrote.

CHAPTER 14

⋆ ⋆ ⋆

Who Am I?

WHEN YOU READ a story or a book, you see the events through someone else's eyes, hear them through someone else's ears. You feel the fictional world through someone else's fingers, smell it through someone else's nose.

That someone else can be one of the characters, or it can be a narrator who's outside the story and knows everything that happens and everything the characters think. The perspective from which the story is told is called the point of view, or POV. When the narrator knows everything, the POV is called third person omniscient. *Omniscient* means "all-knowing." The term *third person* is used because the narrator refers to all the characters in the third person, by name or by the pronouns "he," "she," and "they."

I use the third person omniscient POV in my series The Princess Tales. I love this POV because it feels so powerful. I can drop into anyone's mind at any time. I can show the reader what's going on everywhere, so the reader can know things the main character doesn't know.

Here are snippets from the beginning of *Princess Sonora and the Long Sleep*, which is based on the fairy tale "Sleeping Beauty." In the beginning the narrator zips in and out of the thoughts of a fairy, the baby Sonora, King Humphrey II, and Queen Hermione II. The book opens with the fairy:

> *What a hideous baby, the fairy Arabella thought. She said, "My gift to Sonora is beauty."*

The fairy touches the baby with her wand, and Sonora becomes beautiful and adorable, for a baby. Sonora doesn't like it much.

> *Ouch! It hurt to have your body change shape and to grow hair on your head in ten seconds. Sonora wailed.*
>
> *King Humphrey II of Biddle thought, Why did the fairy do that? As his first-born child—as his lovey dovey oodle boodle baby—she had been fine the way she was.*

That's third person omniscient. It's powerful, but it doesn't bring us, the readers, into the heart of the main character the way another kind of third person POV does. This other kind isn't all-knowing. Instead it sticks with one main character. It reveals only that character's thoughts and only the scenes that character takes part in.

The Birthday Room, which I quoted from on page 59, is told in this sort of third person POV. As we've already seen, Ben, the POV character, is given a room that his parents renovated just for him, for his birthday. This fragment takes place early in the book, just after Ben has seen the room for the first time:

> *Ben nodded. He could tell how pleased his parents were with the gift. . . .*
>
> *"Wow," Ben said again. He didn't want to disappoint them. He loved his parents more than he could say. "Great. This is so great."*

Notice that the narrator doesn't enter the minds of the parents and show us directly that they're pleased. Instead, we find out from Ben that they're pleased, and we take his word for it because he's their son and he knows them well.

The disadvantage of telling a story from one character's POV is that we, the readers, can know only what he or she knows. If, for example, someone is tiptoeing upstairs toward Ben's new room, we'll find out only when Ben does.

The first person POV is similar to this kind of close-focus third person POV. In stories told in the first person, the narrator appears as "I" or "me." The other characters are referred to by name or by the pronouns "he," "she," and "they."

So far all my longer novels have been written from a first person POV. When I started writing *Ella Enchanted*, I was a beginner novelist. I began the book in the close-focus third person, but my critiquing pals kept complaining that Ella wasn't reacting enough to the things that were befalling her. When her mother died, Ella didn't seem to feel the loss deeply enough.

So I switched to first person, and that helped. When I wrote "I," I became Ella. I couldn't ignore her feelings because I was writing as though everything were happening to me.

Of course, the first person POV shares the disadvantage of the close-focus third person POV in that the reader knows only what the POV character knows. In *Ella Enchanted* I got around that somewhat when I invented a magic book that sometimes shows Ella events she couldn't know about in any other way.

First person and third person POVs are the most common ones. But a second person POV is also possible, and I know one book written that way, a young adult novel by A. M. Jenkins, titled *Damage*. In a second person POV the narrator uses the pronoun "you." This is taken from the beginning of the book:

> *It's all yours. Your hands rise, fingers spread, ready to feel the firm scrape of the football, ready to pull it to you, ready to tuck it safely in.*

An amazing thing about point of view is that writing in different POVs feels different. I feel a bit detached from my story when I'm writing in the third person omniscient POV. When I'm writing in the first person, I feel inside the story. I'm right there where the action is taking place, and anything that happens to my POV character happens to me.

Now you try it.

Writing time!

It's early evening. A lion has escaped from the circus. Include as characters the lion tamer, the police chief, a twelve-year-old boy or girl who's home alone, and the lion. You can add more characters. Write the story of the escape and recapture from the third person omniscient POV. Remember that you can reveal the thoughts and feelings of any of your characters, including, of course, the lion.

Next, write two versions of a story about a kidnapping.

The victim can be a child or an adult. The kidnapper can be anyone.

In both versions the story should be told in the first person, first from the POV of the victim, then from the POV of the kidnapper. Remember that when you use the first person, you can include the thoughts and feelings of only your POV character. For the other characters you have to limit yourself to what they say and do. The stories may change from version to version. Let them go where they like.

Have fun!

Save what you wrote.

CHAPTER 15

* * *

Voice

EVERYTHING WRITTEN HAS a voice, from advertisements to warning notices. "Trespassing prohibited" is written in a different voice from "Stay out! That means you!"

Here are the beginnings of three books. Look for differences in the way each one is written.

This is from *Fat Kid Rules the World* by K. L. Going:

> *I'm a sweating fat kid standing on the edge of the subway platform staring at the tracks.*

This is from *My Louisiana Sky* by Kimberly Willis Holt:

> *Folks around Saitter don't understand why parents would name their daughter Tiger. But Daddy says it's because of love.*

This is from *The Wanderer* by Sharon Creech:

The sea, the sea, the sea. It rolled and rolled and called to me. Come in, it said, come in.

Did you catch any differences among the three voices quoted? What were they? Think about them for a few minutes.

To me, the Going quote is gritty and immediate. The Holt quote is direct and full of feeling. The Creech quote is repetitive, giving it rhythm and a hypnotic quality.

Look for other examples of voice. Compare your favorite books. Compare newspapers. Compare advertisements. Listen to the dialogue in movies and on television, and compare. Voice is everywhere. Voice is everything.

Suppose I'd just written "Voice is ubiquitous" instead of "Voice is everywhere." The meaning is the same. I've changed only one word. But the voice is a little different, isn't it?

You have a way of writing that's characteristic of you. Start looking for it. Gather up five or six things you've written. The best samples would be stories and poems, but if you don't have enough of these, then include e-mails and reports for school—just not spelling or math tests!

Read a paragraph here, a paragraph there. Look for

similarities from piece to piece. Are your sentences short or long? Do you notice any words that you use a lot? What about your tone? Is it serious or funny or poetic or even silly?

Do you usually use the same POV? What's your narrator like? Dignified? Chatty? Straightforward? Or does the narrator vary from story to story?

Do you spend many words on your character's thoughts and feelings? Or does action predominate? Or are they equally mixed together?

Do you usually write mysteries? Fantasy? Historical fiction? Contemporary stories set in the everyday world?

Mind you, there are no right or wrong answers to these questions.

In my writing I use questions a lot. In this book, too, I'm tossing them in left and right. I just counted, and I posed seventeen questions in the five paragraphs before this one. That's a lot of questions! Isn't it?

Your voice may change from piece to piece. A story about an earthquake may be written differently from a story about a mission to Mars. And your approach to a fairy tale may be unlike either one.

Your voice may even change within a piece. If you alternate narrators, the voice will vary from one to the other. In a kidnapping story the voice may change a bit from the scene in which the kidnapping is planned to the scene in which it is carried out.

Now, if you can, exchange your writing with the writing of a friend whose judgment you trust, someone who won't be insulting or hurtful. Notice how his is different from your own. Marvel at the differences. Ask yourself the same questions about his writing that you asked about your own.

Don't ask yourself whether your writing is better than his or vice versa.

Take turns with your friend. Describe what you think his voice is like. Show him the places that led you to your conclusions. Then let him tell you if he sees his work the same way you do. Listen while he tells you why and gives you specific examples. Talk about it. Take your time.

Now listen to his description of your voice. Don't say anything until he's finished. Don't try to explain away what he's saying. Absorb it. Store it to think more about later.

Do any of his conclusions surprise you? Don't reject them or embrace them immediately. Let them percolate for a few days. If you're confused about what he's told you, show your writing selections to a second friend, and ask if she agrees with the first friend.

As you write new stories, be aware of your voice.

✦ ✦ ✦ ✦ ✦

Writing time!

This is an exercise in changing voice. Choose at least two of these topics:

- ✦ A sunset
- ✦ A painting
- ✦ A meal
- ✦ A costume
- ✦ A flower
- ✦ A garden
- ✦ A science experiment

Now describe your chosen topics in each of the following ways:

- ✦ Make your words and sentences as long as you can. Use as many words with more than one syllable as you can.
- ✦ Make your words and sentences as short as you can. A few sentence fragments are okay, but don't use only sentence fragments.
- ✦ Use a lot of exclamations.
- ✦ Use a lot of questions.

+ Write your description as though you were explaining to a visitor from another galaxy. The visitor speaks and understands English but has had little experience with things on Earth.
+ Write your description as an advertisement for the thing you're describing.

Read over your descriptions. Notice how different each one is from the others.

Have fun!

Save what you wrote.

* ⋆ *

CHAPTER 16

Happily Ever After—or Not

IN MOST CASES, your story or book should end when its problem is solved, for good or for ill.

Suppose a boy in a story, Noah, has borrowed his father's best watch without permission, and the watch has vanished. It's been lost or stolen, and Noah doesn't know which.

If this is a mystery story, the problem could be solved when the thief is revealed and the watch is recovered and returned to the father's bureau drawer. The father's ignorance of the disappearance and his anticipated anger if he finds out add to the tension along the way.

But suppose the problem of the story isn't really the missing watch but the boy's relationship with his dad. Then the return of the watch won't end the problem unless their relationship is resolved at the same time.

Here's one way it could go: Noah discovers what happened to the watch, and it's gone forever. He confesses to his dad, who's furious. Noah says something like "I know I shouldn't have taken the watch. I know you're going to punish me, and I guess I deserve it. But you're also going to stay mad at me for weeks—you always do—and I don't think that's fair. Didn't you ever do anything bad when you were my age?"

The father is surprised by Noah's words. He remembers getting into trouble and how his mother wouldn't talk to him for days afterward. He relents and forgives his son and maybe goes easy on the punishment. The relationship is strengthened. Problem solved. Story ends.

On the other hand, it might not go so well. Noah may never before have told his dad how he feels, and it takes all his courage to do so now. But his father reacts badly. He decides that his son is being mouthy and doubles Noah's punishment for talking back.

Noah realizes that he can't talk to his dad. He feels like a fool for confessing and swears he won't make that mistake again.

Is the problem solved? Yes. Noah has come to a new understanding of his relationship with his father and has decided on a future course of action.

Is the problem resolved happily? Of course not.

Usually the main character should be changed by the events in your story. Think of your favorite books. I suspect their heroes and heroines have grown in some important way by the end.

Don't worry about making your main character change. Just be aware that she should, and the awareness will seep into your writing.

Character growth often happens naturally. In my first example Noah is likely to be more honest in the future because of his father's sympathetic reaction. Noah is changed by what happened in the story.

But in my second example Noah's honesty is not rewarded, and he's likely to become more secretive. He's changed, too.

Sometimes you may know your story's ending before you start writing. The ending may have come to you first, and you write your story toward it. I love when that happens to me.

But it doesn't happen often. I usually have to struggle to solve the problem. For instance, I had no idea how I was going to end *Ella Enchanted*. At first I thought that one of the stepsisters was going to be the most important character in the ending, aside from Ella. But that didn't work. I agonized and came to the point, which I reach in many of my books, where I wanted to end the story by dropping a bomb on Ella and Char and Hattie and Olive and everybody else!

Naturally I couldn't do that. It would have been a

terrible ending because the ending of a story has to come from within, from the characters and the events that have taken place.

That's why it isn't a good idea to end a story by having the main character wake up from a dream. The dream is an external solution, external to the story. What's more, it makes everything that went before unimportant.

If you don't know how to end a particular story, do what I do. Write notes about the ending. Try out different endings. Use the techniques I suggest in the next chapter, "Stuck!"

When its problem is solved, your story should end. Your main character's crisis is over, and readers will tire quickly of his uneventful post-story life.

Writing time!

Here are two endings exercises:

The first is to write a story toward one of the endings below:

- Maybe they'd meet again someday. Maybe they wouldn't. It didn't matter anymore. She waved good-bye.
- We shook hands.
- My stepmother remained as evil as ever.

✦ And so the story ended where it began, back at the farmhouse.

✦ The judge banged down her gavel. "Innocent!"

By the time you finish, the ending line may no longer suit the story, and you may need a new one, which is fine.

Repeat the exercise with as many of the endings as you like.

The second exercise involves selecting one of your unfinished stories. What problem does your main character have to solve?

If you don't know, think about what it might be, and write a list of possibilities. When you decide which is the problem, go back and strengthen it and the obstacles to solving it. You may have to cut parts of your old story that don't fit anymore. You may have to add new episodes as well.

Now that you know the problem, list five alternative ways to solve it. Be wild. Rule nothing out. If no alternative seems right, list five more. When you get a solution you like, write your story's ending.

Have fun!

Save what you wrote.

Plowing Through

CHAPTER 17

✦ ✦

Stuck!

SOMETIMES I ASK kids why they don't finish their stories. They tell me they get bored or they can't think of anything to happen next.

Then some of them get discouraged and stop writing, when they could have kept on and become future Newbery or National Book Award winners.

They quit because they don't know this truth:

There is no such thing as a perfect book or a perfect story.

Every book in every library on this planet has something wrong with it. It could be something tiny. Maybe a minor character isn't well drawn. Maybe a description goes on too long. Maybe the dialogue is stiff in one spot. There's something wrong with every single one.

No matter how hard we writers try, we will never achieve perfection.

Perfection doesn't matter. No two readers would agree

on whether our book was perfect anyway. Besides, readers care less about perfection and more about connection, getting caught up in a story, caring about the characters.

When you're just starting to write, you may be miles away from perfection, and you may be well aware of it. It's maddening. It's disappointing.

Writing is deceptive. You know how to read. You know what you like in a book and in a story. You know how to write, how to make sentences and paragraphs. So why can't you tell your story in the beautiful way it appears in your mind?

Well, you wouldn't expect yourself to play the trumpet perfectly the first time you picked it up. You wouldn't expect to join the Olympic team the day after you learned to swim.

Writing is a skill, and the more we do it, the better we get at it. I expect to be learning to write till I die. There's always more to learn, and that may be the best thing about being a writer.

There are always challenges. The solutions that were hard-won in the last book may not help in the slightest with the next.

Trouble often begins with the idea of a story. You have a marvelous idea, and you're all fired up. So you start writing, and it fizzles. When this happens, it's because ideas are ideas, and words on paper are words on paper. They're not the same, and they never will be. The purpose of an idea is to get us excited, to get us writing. But once we start, we have to struggle with the words and with the story we've set in motion.

So if you need to, drop your idea and follow your story wherever it takes you.

Unfortunately I often don't know where that is. I get stuck and can't think of anywhere for my story to go. So I'll say to myself that I'm going to write down twelve options, and I'm not going to stop till I get to twelve, even if number four seems perfect. The reason is obvious: Number nine may be just as good as number four, and then I'll have two choices to decide between. Or number eleven may be better than all the rest.

I tell myself that I'm going to write down stupid options as well as excellent ones. I write down the stupid ones because they're brave. This sounds crazy, but it's true. Whenever I start a list, my stupid ideas surge forward, but the usable ones hang back. They're shy, and they want to see how the stupid guys are treated. When they see me behave respectfully to the dopes, they tiptoe out into the open. I snag them and write them down, too.

Also, don't be too quick to reject an idea as stupid. Let it drift around in your mind while you check out its potential.

If the twelve options haven't helped and I've been star-ing blankly at my computer screen or my pad for so long that my eyeballs are ready to fall out, I write junk, the same kind of junk I talked about in Chapter 4, "Eureka!" I may write, "I don't know what I'm doing sitting here. I'd be bet-ter off painting my toenails," but somehow, just the writing, the action after so much frozenness, gets me going again.

Or I may write about the problem that's stumping me, and sometimes I figure it out. Sometimes I don't, but I get so sick of writing notes that I return to my story and the solution comes.

The last trick in my bag is a suggestion from the won-derful kids' book author Doris Orgel. Her advice is to phrase what I'm stuck on as a question, like "What can Ella of *Ella Enchanted* do about the ogres who've captured her?"

I write the question on a Post-It and slap it up on my office door. Then I do my best to forget about it. Mean-while, the back of my mind goes to work. Three hours or three days later the answer arrives.

The thing is, the answer always comes. One way or another, sooner or later, but always.

Writing time!

Melanie is on her way to her graduation. Her parents are with her. They are a happy family. She is graduating with honors. The next day she's leaving for the camp she loves, where she's spent five happy summers. She has lots of friends and a boyfriend at home. She and the boyfriend plan to stay in touch all summer. She has no problems.

List twelve possible disasters that can set her off on a story. Write her story. If you get stuck, list more options. Write notes. Pose the reason you're stuck as a question. Trust that you'll solve the problem. When you do, keep writing.

Have fun!

Save what you wrote.

CHAPTER 18

* ⋆ *

The Operating Room

REVISING IS MY favorite part of writing. When I'm working on a first draft, I feel like a prisoner. I'm in an iron cell with no windows and no doors. Nothing is happening, and I'm trapped. I notice a bit of moisture condensing on the walls, four or five beads of water. Each bead is an idea. I scrape them off and write feverishly till I use them up. Then I wait for more moisture.

But when I finish my first draft, the walls come down. A fragrant breeze wafts by. No more waiting for condensation. All I have to do is make the book better, which can take a long time.

I revise and revise. I may move scenes around or remove some and add others. Characters develop and change. In *Ella Enchanted* I rewrote the ending a dozen times before I got it right. In an early version of *Cinderellis and the Glass Hill* the three horses could talk, but in the published book they're mute. In *The Two Princesses of Bamarre* the sorcerer

Rhys went from evil to good when I revised.

I wrote the beginning of *The Two Princesses of Bamarre* at least a billion times. This is only a slight exaggeration. When I started the book, I thought I was writing a novelization of the fairy tale "The Twelve Dancing Princesses." Here's an early beginning:

> *Fable has multiplied us. Perhaps the hall of mirrors where we danced is to blame. Instead of twenty-four, we were only six. Three princesses. Three princes.*
>
> *There was always one soldier. Fable did not multiply him. Fable couldn't, not such a one as he.*

I adored it. But the story didn't go that way. Here's a later beginning:

> *I am Bella, the princesses' nanny, and this is the princesses' tale. I know some of it because I was there. The rest I pieced together afterward.*

Here's another one:

> *When Bram died his foolish death, I was fighting in King Eldred's army, fighting for Eldred and Bamar, killing lads and men who had never done me harm.*

Here's the actual beginning of *The Two Princesses of Bamarre*:

> *Out of a land laid waste*
> *To a land untamed,*
> *Monster ridden,*
> *The lad Drualt led*
> *A ruined, ragtag band.*
> *In his arms, tenderly,*
> *He carried Bruce,*
> *The child king,*
> *First ruler of Bamarre.*
>   *So begins Drualt, the epic poem of Bamarre's greatest hero, our kingdom's ideal.*

Some of the earlier beginnings may be more beautifully written than the one that appears in the book, but they didn't set my story off to the right start, and that was why I had to change them. I didn't find my story instantly, so I revised repeatedly as the plot took shape.

You will sometimes write paragraphs of staggering loveliness. You will! Probably you already have. You'll want to have those paragraphs tattooed on your forehead where everyone will see them.

Then you'll discover that they don't help tell your story.

Do not *do not* DO NOT <u>DO NOT</u> **DO NOT** bend your story to accommodate your brilliant words.

Revising and cutting take courage and self-confidence. You have to believe that you will write equally brilliant prose again. And you will. There's no doubt about it. And some of your new brilliant prose will have to be revised or cut. But some will actually fit your story. Hallelujah!

I, too, save everything I write, so in the computer file for each of my books or short stories I keep a document titled "Extra," and I park my peerless but useless prose there. *Extra* is my treasure lode. I can mine it, and so can biographers!

Here's a strategy I use in writing a first draft or in revising when I take my story down a path I'm not sure of and I don't want to lose what I already have.

On my computer I save my story in its old version. Say I save it as "elves 1." Then I save it again as "elves 2." I go to the spot where my alteration begins and start writing. If all goes well, I won't need the old version, but if my new idea fizzles, I haven't lost anything. By the time I've finished writing and revising a book, I may be up to "elves 50"!

To do the same thing in longhand, be careful not to erase your old version. Don't cross out. Don't throw away the old pages. Just draw an arrow to fresh paper, write a version number, and keep going. When you're all finished, you can cut away the parts you don't need and save them somewhere else.

My books are often too long. When I start cutting, I discover tons of words and sentences and whole paragraphs the book could do marvelously well without. In *Fairest* I wanted to show the reader that Ivi was not a good queen, so I piled on example after example of her misrule. "Enough!" my editor said after two or three. "We get the message." So I snipped off several unnecessary examples, and the book got better. The pace picked up, and the action barreled along.

So you learn from revising, and you get to know your style better and—gulp—your faults better.

When you've finished writing a draft of a story, never read it over again immediately. Put it aside. If you can, wait a few weeks before you look at it again. If you can't, wait a day.

You can't be objective immediately. If you're like me, you'll love it, and you won't see the places that need fixing. Or you may hate it, as I can do, too, when I'm feeling low. But both reactions are unreliable.

When you delay the rereading, you get some distance, and you can see what's really there on the page. Your revisions will be better for the wait.

I'm compelled to add this: If you absolutely despise revising, don't let your revulsion make you stop writing.

You'll get better even if you just keep starting new stories and never revise. But know that someday, if you're serious about writing fiction, you're going to have to face the revising beast.

Rewriting time!

Pick out one of your stories. Go through it, revising and fixing as you go. You may do some cutting, but be sure not to drop a single important idea. You may find that you need to add a sequence or two. For example, if you're not sure why a character is behaving in a particular way, or if you can't picture the action as you read the words, you probably need to expand some parts of your story.

When it comes to cutting, cast a suspicious eye on your adjectives and adverbs. Try eliminating each one and see if you can live without it. Read the sentence over and decide. Some adjectives and adverbs will be essential, but some will just be taking up space, and your writing will be stronger without them.

Now read the piece over. What do you think?

Have fun!

Save what you revised.

* ✦ *

CHAPTER 19

Writers' Groups and Other Helpers

T HERE ARE TWO KINDS of writers, those who share their works in progress and those who don't show a word to anyone until they're done. I'm in the first category. I criticize my own work as much as I can, but I also need outside help. I want to be sure I'm saying what I mean to say. I think I'm being funny, but am I? Is the surprise I set up surprising? How can I fix my ending?

You can form a writers' group. Then again, you don't have to. If you're a solitary writer, you should continue to write the way that's most comfortable for you. If you do form a group, there can be as many of you as, say, seven and as few as two. Group members can be friends or relatives, your age or not.

If it isn't possible to start a group, you can show your stories to trusted friends, teachers, and relatives.

At the moment my writers' group (not my workshop with the kids) has only two members, the wonderful young adult writer Joan Abelove and me. The help Joan gives me is sublime.

Not all writers' groups operate the same way. Joan and I e-mail our works in progress to each other. We print out each other's pages and write on them. When we get together, we go over the comments to make sure they're understood.

In some groups the members read a chapter or a short story aloud to one another when they meet. Then they comment on what they've heard. Or they may hand out the work they need help with right on the spot.

When I started writing in 1987, before I'd met Joan, I formed a writers' group with other beginners. None of us knew much, but we tried our best to help one another. We may not have been experienced writers, but we were experienced readers. We knew what we liked, and when something went wrong in a story, we offered our opinions on why.

The criticism wasn't always useful. Even today Joan's critiques sometimes don't help me. I'm better now at recognizing which criticism I can use and which I can't. In the early days I tried out just about every suggestion that came my way. If it helped, I'd leave it in. If it didn't, I'd take it out. Either way, I learned something.

What I'm about to say goes for writers' group members or for anyone you go to for critical help: If someone says that your story is lousy or that you can't write to save yourself, you must never, ever show your precious writing to that person again. She doesn't deserve it. Erase her words from your memory banks.

If this person is in your writers' group, you and the other members must deal with her. When she dumps on someone, you all have to protect that writer by assuring him that his story is *not* terrible. You have to tell the one who has done the dumping that her comments must be constructive or she has to leave the group. And you have to mean it.

My buddy Joan's criticism is always constructive. Still, even though I've known her for years, even though she likes my writing, I'm always nervous when she tells me what she thinks. Sometimes I start commenting on her work before she can get going on mine because I want to delay the awful moment as long as possible.

There's a good way to take writing criticism and a not-so-good way. The good way is to just listen. Don't say a word. You're taking in the criticism. You're memorizing it so you can consider it, now and later. Take notes, so you're sure to remember. Stifle thoughts that the one who's giving the critique has totally misunderstood you and is a complete idiot. Give the criticism a chance.

When you go back to your story, recall the criticism, and experiment to see if it's useful.

The not-so-good way to take criticism is to argue about it or explain it away. If you do that, whoever is giving the comment will probably say, "Uh-huh. Okay." He isn't going to fight with you. You'll feel that you set the matter straight, and you'll lose the value of his advice. And he may not offer it so readily next time. After all, would you?

Sometimes you'll be certain that the criticism is wrong. Even when you are, don't disagree. Listen anyway. The person is trying to help you. It's no skin off your nose to be polite.

When you go back to your story and think hard about the criticism, you may sometimes find that you don't understand what was said. That's the time to speak up. Call the person or wait till you see him again, and ask. You can discuss the criticism then, since you've had time to digest it. Tell him you're not sure what bothered him. He'll be delighted to try to explain.

When there are three or more in a writers' group, it's helpful to see if more than one person has a particular reaction. If only one person sees a problem, there may not be one. But if two or three people think something's wrong, you should take that pretty seriously. If there are only two in your group, you may want to show the part in question to someone else and ask if she agrees with the criticism you've already gotten.

When it's your turn to criticize, be honest. Don't pretend something's wonderful if you think it isn't. However, if you hate someone's story, don't put it that way. Say where the story went wrong for you. First mention the things you liked. Then move on to the problems.

Concentrate on the big stuff, the story stuff, rather than spelling, grammar, and punctuation. Did a character do something that wasn't logical? Did a character act in a way that wasn't characteristic, so to speak? For example, did a mean character become nice without any explanation?

Does the scene shift to a new location, but you don't understand how the story got there? Does the story reveal only what's seen and never what's heard or smelled or touched? Was there a stretch when you got bored? Did the hero get out of his predicaments too easily?

These aren't the only important questions. Each story will suggest new ones. Just as you'll become a better writer with practice, so you'll also become a better critic.

During the nine years it took me to get a book accepted for publication, when my stories were being rejected by every publisher in the known universe, writers' groups got me through. My pals were my audience. They encouraged me. I told them about my rejections and they told me about theirs, and we found comfort in sharing. They helped me become a better writer, and their praise let me know that I was becoming one.

I've discovered in my writing workshop that I enjoy writing in a group. I make up exercises before we get together (many of them are in this book), and then we do them. I didn't think I would be, but I'm as comfortable writing with the group as I am when I write alone at home.

When I say that we write in a group, I don't mean we write together, with different people contributing words and sentences to one cooperative story. We each write our own stories, but we do so in one another's company.

If you try writing together, it will probably be helpful to pick a timekeeper, someone whose job will be to say how long you're going to write for. In the workshop we usually write in twenty-minute stretches, more or less.

It's also good to pick someone to crack the whip. What happens sometimes is that we'll all be writing and someone will say, "What should I name a character who owns a monkey?" Everybody starts suggesting names, and we start talking about how important the right name is, and ten minutes have gone by and nobody's written a word. So then I, since I'm in charge, remind everybody to get back to writing.

You need someone like me, a boss.

✦ ✦ ✦ ✦ ✦

Writing time!

J.R.R. Tolkien invented the word *mathom* in his *Lord of the Ring*s trilogy. A mathom is an object you don't want but can't stand to give away or throw away. Do you have a mathom? Most of us do. It's a great word, and the English language needs it.

You're going to invent a word, too. The people in your writers' group can invent their own words as well, if you like.

First you need a concept for which there is no word, so far as you know. Spend a few days, while you're going about your regular life, searching for such a concept. For example, my husband thinks there should be a word for expiring of thirst, just as *starving* means expiring of hunger.

When you think of a concept, write it down, and see if you can make up a word for it. When I did this exercise, my concept was the experience of having a great idea and forgetting it before you can write it down. I came up with the fancy word *lethescriptosis*.

When you've invented a word, start using it in conversation. If anyone asks, and you're feeling mischievous, give the definition, but don't say you made it up. See if it catches on.

Have fun!

Save what you wrote.

Digging Deeper

··*

CHAPTER 20

Show and Tell

WRITERS ARE OFTEN advised to show, not tell. You need to do both.

When you show, you slow the action to a crawl. You imagine the moment in your story and put down every important thing that happens, using tons of detail. You include dialogue and the POV character's thoughts and feelings and the sensations I talked about in Chapter 6, "Noticing."

When you tell, you summarize the action. You don't stop for details or dialogue or thoughts and feelings or sensations. Events fly by when you're telling.

Traditional fairy tales are often good examples of telling. This excerpt is from "The Sleeping Beauty in the Wood" in *The Blue Fairy Book*, edited by Andrew Lang:

> *There were formerly a king and a queen, who were so sorry that they had no children; so sorry that it cannot*

*be expressed. They went to all the waters in the world;
vows, pilgrimages, all ways were tried, and all to no
purpose.*

*At last, however, the Queen had a daughter. There
was a very fine christening; and the Princess had for her
god-mothers all the fairies they could find in the whole
kingdom (they found seven), that every one of them might
give her a gift, as was the custom of fairies in those days.*

The first paragraph covers years. We don't see the king
and the queen weeping over their childlessness. We don't
accompany them on their pilgrimages or hear them take
even a single vow.

The second paragraph doesn't cover as much time, but
it's still telling. We don't see the christening take place or
meet the fairies.

An example of showing comes from my *Dave at Night*.
Dave has recently arrived at the orphanage, and his prefect,
Mr. Meltzer, takes him to meet the orphanage superinten-
dent, Mr. Bloom:

*Mr. Bloom was huge. His head and chest loomed
over his desk like the Hebrew Home for Boys loomed
over Broadway. He pushed back his chair and stood up.
Scraping against the wall on the way, he walked around*

to my side of his desk and bent down to inspect me through thick spectacles. He smiled, showing a million teeth.

He looked up at Mr. Meltzer, who was leaning against the door so I couldn't get out. "What's his name?"

He could have asked me. Didn't he think I knew my own name?

We're right there in Mr. Bloom's office. We see Mr. Bloom. We hear him speak. We read Dave's thoughts. That's showing.

Another difference between the two selections is that the fairy-tale paragraphs are presented in the third person by an anonymous narrator, and the *Dave at Night* paragraphs are presented in the first person by Dave himself. The sort of narrator, however, doesn't really matter for show and tell. An anonymous narrator can show, and a first person narrator can tell.

Telling is like looking down from the window of an airplane. The world rushes by. Only the biggest landmarks stand out: a river, a mountain, a suburb. We can't make out the rowboat in the river, the bear on the mountain, the boy in the suburban backyard.

Showing is like being on the ground. We see the rowboat. We see that it was once painted red but that most of the paint has peeled off. We see the muscles bulging in the arms of the rower. We see the passenger take soda cans out of the cooler. We notice the beads of water condensing on the cans. We don't see the whole river. We don't even see the rapids around the next bend, although we may hear the roar of the water.

What you want is a writer's telescope, so you can increase or decrease the magnification: increase to show, decrease to tell. In the example from *Dave at Night* I could have increased the magnification and said whether Mr. Bloom was bald or had thick red hair. I could have said what Mr. Meltzer's hands were doing, whether they were in his pockets or folded across his chest. I could have revealed how close Dave was to Mr. Bloom's desk or if he was biting his lips.

In fact I could have put in a dozen more details. I could have said that Mr. Bloom's shirt collar was too tight, and the skin above it looked chafed. I could have mentioned that Mr. Meltzer's brown tweed jacket was buttoned wrong. And on and on. But if I went into all that, the reader would fall asleep.

So how do you know what to put in and what to leave out? How do you know how much magnification is right?

In general, you want to put in details that reveal character, or move the story along, or establish the setting or the atmosphere. The best details do more than one at the same time.

Usually, when we write, we mix showing and telling together. We tell a little here, show a little there. Often the two are so closely entwined that you can hardly separate them. This is from the opening of *Ella Enchanted*. I've put the showing parts *in italics*, so you can see which is which:

That fool of a fairy Lucinda did not intend to lay a curse on me. She meant to bestow a gift. When I cried inconsolably through my first hour of life, my tears were her inspiration. *Shaking her head sympathetically at Mother, the fairy touched my nose. "My gift is obedience. Ella will always be obedient. Now stop crying, child."*

I stopped.

Father was away on a trading expedition as usual, but our cook, Mandy, was there. She and Mother were horrified, but no matter how they explained it to Lucinda, they couldn't make her understand the terrible thing she'd done to me. I could picture the argument: *Mandy's freckles standing out sharper than usual, her frizzy gray hair in disarray, and her double chin shaking with anger; Mother, still and intense, her brown curls damp from labor, the laughter gone from her eyes.*

But suppose I'd done the first paragraph all in showing. It might have gone like this:

> *Lucinda frowned as she watched me sobbing in Mother's arms. She took a step back and covered her ears with her gloved hands. "Will the babe never stop crying?" Shaking her head sympathetically at Mother, the fairy came close again and touched my nose. "My gift is obedience. Ella will always be obedient. Now stop crying, child."*

In this new version we gain the information that Ella is in her mother's arms and that Lucinda is wearing gloves. But we lose the judgments that Lucinda is a fool and that the gift is a curse.

Here's another quality of telling: It delivers conclusions directly. In showing, we're led to the conclusion the writer wants us to reach, but we have to draw it ourselves.

Let's look again at the passage from *Dave at Night*:

> *Mr. Bloom was huge. His head and chest loomed over his desk like the Hebrew Home for Boys loomed over Broadway. He pushed back his chair and stood up. Scraping against the wall on the way, he walked around to my side of his desk and bent down to inspect me*

through thick spectacles. He smiled, showing a million teeth.

He looked up at Mr. Meltzer, who was leaning against the door so I couldn't get out. "What's his name?"

He could have asked me. Didn't he think I knew my own name?

I don't tell the reader what to think of Mr. Bloom, but I don't leave the outcome to chance either. I put in enough evidence to ensure that the reader will decide that Mr. Bloom doesn't respect children.

If I hadn't told the reader that Lucinda was a fool, I could have shown it, just as I did with Mr. Bloom. But it would have taken a lot more words.

Telling is faster, while showing pulls you into the story more. Usually a novel will do more showing, and a fable will do more telling. Which is better, showing or telling? Well, which is better, a novel or a fable?

They're both fine.

Go to a book you like. Read a page. Is it all telling or all showing, or a mix? Which parts are which?

Writing time!

You're going to use showing to write about yourself doing something ordinary. Like this:

I'm brushing my teeth, even though it's the middle of the afternoon and I haven't eaten anything. I take the toothbrush, which is gray and white, out of the mug it stands in, being careful to select my toothbrush and not my husband's (which I've done a few times—an icky mistake!).

The toothbrush's bristles are multicolored, and I wonder why the manufacturer made them that way. I lift the toothpaste out of the same mug that holds the toothbrushes, and I unscrew the top. I'm surprised by the number of times I have to twist.

The tube is almost empty. I massage its end, pushing tiny bumps of toothpaste ahead of my fingers.

And so on.

Now you do it. Write about getting up in the morning or getting dressed or eating lunch or riding the bus to school. Whichever you pick, I want you to write at least a page, and I want you not to have finished the description by the time you get to the bottom of the page. When I wrote about brushing my teeth, I couldn't just sit at my computer and imagine the process. No, I had to actually brush them in order to include everything. You probably will have to do whatever activity you are writing about, too.

This exercise is a good time to practice shutting up that

negative whiner in your head. I couldn't write great literature describing myself brushing my teeth. Maybe somebody
could, but not I. And I'm not worried about it.

You shouldn't worry either. It's just an exercise, just
practice.

I try to regard all my writing that way, as an exercise on
the way to becoming a better writer. Somebody else can
decide if it's literature.

Doing this exercise isn't very different from writing
more important things, the fiction that may turn into literature. A lot of writing is plodding, pedestrian, even trivial.
But if you can describe making a sandwich, you can describe
spreading a special mustard on the bread, a mustard that
makes the person who eats it able to understand the language of animals. You can describe the texture of the mustard. Maybe it's extra grainy. Maybe it's a little greasy.
Maybe it's hard to wash off the knife.

See? Out of lunch you spin magic.

In this next exercise think of someone you know who's
nice, a decent person. Then think of someone who's not nice.
Make up new names for them. Imagine them imprisoned
together in the dungeon of a fairy-tale castle.

Use showing to write what happens. Don't tell the
reader who's nice and who's not. Instead, show the rotten
person being rotten and the nice person being nice.

Does either of them get out alive? Both of them? Neither?

Show us!

Have fun!

Save what you wrote.

CHAPTER 21

* ⋆ *

Abracadabra!

*S*AID IS A MAGICAL WORD. Boring maybe, but magical nonetheless. It's magical because it disappears. It becomes invisible.

What I'm about to tell you may differ from what your teachers have told you. Your teachers may ask you to use lots of variants on *said* instead of *said* over and over. The reason is probably that they want you to vary your vocabulary and not use the same word repeatedly.

That's often fine advice, but not when it comes to *said* in stories. *Asked* is about as good as *said* if the line of dialogue is a question. *Asked* also disappears. And so does *added*, if it's used when it makes sense and not used too much.

But you should almost never write, "'Where did you put the aardvark?' she *queried*," or "'Don't you hate aardvarks?' he *questioned*."

Query and *question* call attention to themselves and away from your story. The reader sees the question mark and knows that the character is querying or questioning.

Avoid other noticeable words, like *affirm*, *allege*, *articulate*, *assert*, *asseverate* (a word I'd never heard of before I started writing this), *aver*, *avow*, *claim*, *comment*, *confabulate*, *contend*, *declare*, *express*, *hint*, *mention*, *observe*, *opine*, *pronounce*, *profess*, *remark*, *utter*, *voice*. I don't mean that you shouldn't ever use these perfectly fine words. I just mean don't use them as a substitute for *said*.

Try this: Pull out an old story. Above your substitutes for *said*, write *said*. Read your dialogue both ways. Which is better?

There are a few exceptions to this rule. It's okay, even good, to use a *said* alternative that indicates volume. You can write, "We have to get out of here," Tim *whispered*, or "We have to get out of here," Gillian *shouted* (or *yelled* or *screamed* or *screeched*). These verbs are okay because you're giving the reader new information when you use them. But don't make your characters whisper or holler just to avoid using *said*.

It's also okay to use a substitute for *said* if you're being funny. Here's an example:

> "*I despise and detest simple locutions,*" he *asseverated*.
> "*Aw, shut your trap,*" she *growled*.

And it's fine to use another word if you can get away with it, if your story simply reads better that way.

Fashions in writing change. If you look at an old classic, you'll see lots of uninvisible speech verbs. I just looked at *Jane Eyre* by Charlotte Brontë, which was published in 1847, and I found a place where a main character *recommenced* rather than *said*! I also looked at my favorite novel, *Pride and Prejudice*, by Jane Austen, published in 1817. I discovered that Austen uses *cried* for *said* so often that *cried* becomes invisible.

Take a peek into a few of the books you love, the ones written in the last fifty years. Do you see words like *exclaimed* or *queried* or *interjected*? I don't think you do.

Because these days *said* is beautiful.

Writing time!

This is a dialogue exercise. Pick one of the two below, or do both:

+ A brother and sister have been left on a street corner in a part of town they don't know. Write down their conversation about what to do.
+ A spaceship from Earth approaches a planet that has been little explored by humans. The ship is crewed by two space explorers. They talk about how to make

contact with the natives, who are known to be intelligent. Write down their discussion.

Turn the exercises into stories, if you like.
Have fun!
Save what you wrote.

* ⭑ *

CHAPTER 22

I'd Recognize Her with
My Eyes Closed

M UCH AS I LIKE the word *said*, I love being able to skip
it entirely. Sometimes you can show your reader who's
talking without naming a name. And when you can, it's neat.

In *The Wish* Nina is one of the popular girls. The reader
meets her when the main character, Wilma, takes her dog
with her to a sleepover. This is what Nina says about bringing
the dog: "It's pretty weird, Wilma. Five points off for
strange behavior."

Nina often gives points or takes points away. Nobody
else in the book does it. So pretty soon the reader knows
who's talking when *points* appears, and it becomes unnecessary to identify Nina.

What's the good of this?

Well, in the last chapter I said that *said* is invisible.
Maybe I should have said it's ignorable, because it's still
there, taking up space without contributing to plot or character or anything else. It just sits there, and if you can do

without it, so much the better.

Speech mannerisms usually tell you about the character. Nina's a judgmental kid, and her point system reveals that.

Speech mannerisms please the reader. They make him feel in the know. Hey, that's Nina, he thinks. I'd know her anywhere. And he burrows deeper into the story.

So, what other speech mannerisms are there?

I figure you know someone who finishes your sentences for you. You pause to take a breath, and she wraps up what you were going to say. That's a speech mannerism.

You may have run into someone who always starts whatever he's going to say with "Listen!" He's notified you that he desperately wants your attention. That's a speech mannerism.

I recently met someone who peppered her speech with "You know what?" She'd ask the question and then answer it. She was an angry person, and usually the answer was hostile, as in "You know what? You're an idiot." Or "You know what? This food is lousy."

On pages 53–54 I gave an example of unnatural speech in which two kids are talking about a fire in school. Here's a repeat of the first two paragraphs:

> *"My first suspicion of trouble came during language arts when my nose detected a whiff of smoke,"* *Abigail said.*

"That whiff must have frightened you. Did you realize immediately that the cause was a fire?"

I said you should avoid this kind of dialogue.

Well, you should avoid it almost always, but stiff, awkward dialogue is fine if you use it to be funny, or if your character is stiff and awkward and that's the way she really talks.

You don't want to give speech mannerisms to all your characters, or your readers will go nuts, trying to keep them straight. And not all your characters will suggest mannerisms to you.

Writing time!

From now on, pay attention to the way people say what they say, and listen for speech mannerisms. Maybe a teacher uses one particular expression when he's mad at the class. Maybe he has another expression reserved for when he's especially pleased. Maybe your little brother has picked up a phrase that he repeats constantly.

When you notice a speech mannerism, write it down. Then write how the mannerism makes you feel. Speculate about the reasons the person might have the mannerism, and write your ideas down. There can be different reasons. For instance, the person who finishes sentences for you might do it because she's very sympathetic and wants to help you along with whatever you're trying to say. Or she might be impatient and doesn't want to wait for you to drag the whole thing out.

For each mannerism you notice, do a character questionnaire about a made-up person who has that mannerism. The made-up person can be a lot like the real person or doesn't have to be.

Use the characters (or character) in a story. See if the mannerism influences the way the story goes.

If you can't find a real person with a speech mannerism, invent a mannerism and a character to go with it, using the character questionnaire. Write a story about the character, making sure you include some dialogue that reveals the mannerism.

Have fun!

Save what you wrote.

* ⋆ *

CHAPTER 23

Speaking Body Language

THERE'S MORE TO DIALOGUE than just speech, in fiction and in real life. While you talk, you may scratch behind your left ear. You rub your hands together. You look down at the ground. You smile. You nod. You watch the sun set. You pick at a scab on your arm.

The movements a person makes when she's with other people are called body language. Body language can communicate as eloquently as words, and sometimes more truthfully. It can be easy to speak a lie, but it's hard to act one out.

I'll bet that at some time or other you've tried to hide that you were angry with someone but gave yourself away without meaning to. Maybe you didn't smile when ordinarily you would have. Maybe the person was someone you always greeted with a hug, but you held your body stiff and ended the hug too quickly.

Here's an example of body language from my novel *The*

Wish. Wilma is the first person POV character. The other characters are her friends, and except for one of them, they're all mad at her.

> *Daphne listened the way you'd listen to a friend, nodding, smiling, frowning in all the right places. BeeBee said "far out" once, and "oh, wow" once, but mostly she fiddled with her hair, winding a strand around her finger and unwinding it. Nina crossed her arms and stared at me without saying anything. Ardis made clicking noises with her tongue every so often, like everything I said was garbage. She never looked at me, just stared up at the ceiling.*

You can tell, can't you, that Daphne's the one who isn't mad. That BeeBee's sort of in the middle. And Nina and Ardis are very, very mad, even though neither of them says a word.

Body language is powerful, so you want to get it working for you in your stories. Remember the conversation between the cousins Abigail and Brynn on page 54:

> "I smelled smoke in language arts," Abigail said. "Not much. Just a whiff."
> "That must have been scary. Did you know right

away it was a fire?"

"Uh-uh. Language arts is next door to the science lab. There are weird smells all the time."

"Tell me about it. When did you realize what was going on?"

"Well, Ms. Montolio's our principal. I knew something was wrong when her voice came out of the PA system. She wouldn't do that over a science experiment."

We don't have a clue to what they're doing. They could be playing Ping-Pong or roasting marshmallows. We don't know how they feel about each other, except that they're on speaking terms.

Let's fill in the blanks. Let's imagine that they're sitting on the grass in Abigail's backyard, waiting to be called in for dinner. Let's imagine that Brynn is two years younger than her cousin. She looks up to Abigail and wants to impress her. Abigail, on the other hand, thinks Brynn is boring.

Now watch. I'm going to add in body language and a few thoughts without changing a word either of them says.

"I smelled smoke in language arts," Abigail said. "Not much. Just a whiff." She scratched a mosquito bite.

Brynn leaned in close, but she failed to get Abigail

to meet her eyes. *"That must have been scary."*

Abigail moved six inches away.

Brynn moved closer again. "Did you know right away it was a fire?"

"Uh-uh." Abigail fell silent.

Brynn cocked her head, waiting. The silence lasted a full two minutes.

Abigail shrugged. "Language arts is next door to the science lab. There are weird smells all the time."

Brynn nodded enthusiastically. "Tell me about it. When did you realize what was going on?"

"Well . . ." Abigail looked at her watch. "Ms. Montolio's our principal. I knew something was wrong when her voice came out of the PA system. She wouldn't do that over a science experiment." She stood up and turned to go into the house.

What do you think? Are you starting to care about these characters, especially Brynn? It could become a story this way, beginning, perhaps, with Brynn excited about visiting her cousin, full of hope for their friendship.

Writing time!

Take out the dialogue exercises I asked you to save, from Chapter 11, "Talking." If you did more than one exercise, choose one. If, alas, you can't find your exercise, do it again, or use a section of undiluted dialogue from one of your stories, or make up a page of new dialogue. Decide where the conversation is taking place, and expand the situation. Decide who your characters are, and flesh out the relationship between them. For example, Nadia could be eighty-six years old, and Kelsey could be eighty-four, living together in a nursing home. They could have gotten along well all their lives, or their relationship could be one long argument.

Whatever you decide, add actions, body language, and thoughts to their dialogue. You can change what they say if you need to.

If this leads to a story, go with it. If not, that's okay.

Feel free to do this with any of your other saved dialogues.

Have fun!

Save what you wrote.

* ⋆ *

CHAPTER 24

Method Writing

WE FICTION WRITERS have to write about things that have never happened to us, and we have to make them believable. Sometimes we need to write about emotions we've never felt. How do we do it? How do you do it?

Actors do something similar. An actor may play a slave or a pirate or an extraterrestrial. I saw a play in which a woman had the part of a dog, and she didn't even wear a dog costume.

How do actors do this?

Well, I'm sure the actor who played the dog spent time watching dogs. She may also have used a technique called method acting.

In method acting an actor remembers events and feelings in his own life that are similar to what his character goes through. For example, an actor playing a murderer has (we hope) never killed anyone. But he probably has killed a few mosquitoes, maybe a cockroach or two, several ants.

You have, too, I'm sure. When you've slapped at a mosquito and killed it, have you ever thought about the life you just snuffed out? You may have felt pity and irritation at the same time. Irritation because you don't like mosquitos, and why did it pick you to bite? Pity because you know that the mosquito didn't mean to hurt you and it was an innocent creature just doing what it was built to do.

The actor may use these kinds of recollections to deepen his portrayal of a murderer.

An actor who plays an extraterrestrial almost certainly isn't one, but maybe he once visited a country where he didn't know the language or the customs. You may have recently moved to a new neighborhood and a new school. People do things differently here, and you don't know anyone. Don't you feel a bit like an extraterrestrial?

You can do what the stage and screen stars do. You can use these similar experiences to build your characters. You can be a method writer.

Writing time!

Use method writing for one or more of these possibilities:

+ Your main character is a spy. You've never been a real spy, but I suspect you've once or twice tried to find out information you weren't supposed to know. Probably you've overheard things not intended for your ears. Maybe you've even for some reason pretended to be someone's friend when you really weren't. These are spylike experiences. Use them and the feelings you had then to tell a story about the spy.

+ Your main character is Rapunzel when the prince comes along. Or your main character is the prince when he meets Rapunzel. They begin to talk. She starts falling in love with him, and he starts falling in love with her. From the point of view of either of them, write about falling in love.

You may never have experienced romantic love, but you've fallen *in like* with friends. And you love people in your family. You love your pet. Draw on these experiences to tell the story.

+ Your main character is the world-famous inventor of a time-travel machine. To enter his or her persona, think about inspired moments you've had. Think about times you've been recognized for any sort of achievement. Tell a story from the inventor's first person POV.

Have fun!
Save what you wrote.

✦ ✦ ✦

Writing Funny, Writing Punny

YOU CAN BE A WONDERFUl writer and never write a funny line. Many fine writers have long and successful careers writing serious mysteries, adventure stories, dramas, romances—all kinds of books. These writers may have terrific senses of humor in person, if not in print.

But if you want to write funny stories, this chapter may help you. I say *may* help because humor is slippery. What I think is hysterical may strike you as not at all funny, may even seem stupid to you. You and I both may have thought something was funny a year ago. But when we remember it, it no longer seems the slightest bit amusing.

When you try the exercises at the end of this chapter, it's possible that nothing funny will emerge. Don't worry. You may find yourself being a riot another time, when you're not thinking about it. Humor can't be forced.

Here's a joke. You may know it. It's ancient.

Farmer Brown has two horses. He can't tell them apart.

Their heads are the same size. Both have bushy manes and tails. They're both sweet tempered and hard workers. Finally Farmer Brown decides to measure them, hoping that one is a little taller than the other. He measures each horse, and *bingo!* The brown horse is four inches taller than the white horse.

If you found this joke funny it's because the punch line is unexpected. Most jokes depend on surprise. Think of a few. They're probably funny because you can't see the punch line coming.

Surprise works in other kinds of humor, too, not just jokes. A frail old lady with smelly feet is unexpected and humorous. But a football player with smelly feet isn't funny. He's ordinary.

In this passage from *Princess Sonora and the Long Sleep*, our notion of baby behavior is turned upside down, and the result is amusing—I hope:

> *The Royal Nursemaids couldn't get used to Sonora.*
> *It was so strange to change the diaper of a baby who was*
> *reading a book, especially a baby who blushed and said,*
> *"I'm so sorry to bother you with my elimination."*

However, not all humor depends on surprise. Some things—toe jam, for instance—are intrinsically funny, at least to some people. Farts are endlessly funny to some. Food can be funny: Imagine green-mold-and-alligator-eyeball stew. Can you think of other items that are funny all by themselves? Let your mind go. In humor of this sort, *nothing* is stupid.

Some humor is fueled by the expected, not the un-expected. Amelia Bedelia, for example, is a character who tends to misunderstand what's happening and to act on her misunderstanding. As we read, we discover that when she gets mixed up, funny things happen. So if events start shaping up in a way that Amelia Bedelia is likely to misunderstand, we start grinning ahead of time, in anticipation. And whatever mess Amelia Bedelia winds up causing is funnier because of our anticipation.

Humor is deepened when it's connected to something serious. At one point in *Ella Enchanted* Ella's parrot, Chock, commands her to kiss him. But he keeps flying away before she can. The result is a funny scene, made funnier by the underlying terrible curse of obedience.

Along these lines, have you ever noticed that personal disasters often turn into funny stories when they're safely over? I once heard the children's book writer and illustrator Patricia Polacco tell about a plane trip during which her suitcase melted and her white fur coat was destroyed. It must have been awful at the time, but everyone who heard the story was gasping with laughter.

Puns are a more intellectual kind of humor with almost no emotional depth. They depend on meaning, and they'll never make you fall out of your chair laughing. You may groan instead of laugh, but they're still funny.

Robin, the hero in *The Fairy's Return*, has a calling to be a punster. When he meets Princess Lark, he tells her puns related to nobility and royalty. Here are a few of them:

> *Why is a king like a yardstick? They're both rulers.*
> *Which rank of nobility is best at math? The count.*
> *Why do noblemen like to stare? Because they're peers.*

I can tell you how I thought these up. First I listed all the words I could think of that have to do with nobility, royalty, castles, or court life. My thesaurus and encyclopedia helped me. Then I stared at the list and let my mind click along. In particular I looked for words that have double meanings, even if the other meaning is spelled differently.

For *king* I came up with *sovereign*, *ruler*, *sire*, *highness*, *majesty*, *monarch*, *rex*. *Sovereign* also means a certain kind of coin. But many people wouldn't know that, and nothing is funny when your audience doesn't know what you're talking about.

Ruler has two meanings, and everyone knows them,

making it a better candidate. Another advantage was that both *ruler* and *king* are nouns (*sovereign* and *king* are, too). It's especially hard to develop a pun using different parts of speech—a noun and a verb, for instance.

The next step was to put *ruler* and *king* together and to do it without giving the joke away. "Why is a king like a measuring instrument?" is no good, because the answer is obvious. "Why may a king have three feet?" isn't quite right. There might be a better way to phrase it, but the best I could find is the one I used: "Why is a king like a yardstick?"

A few years ago my husband got us on a favorite-foods punning jag. He started it with: What's a plumber's favorite vegetable? The answer: leeks. Get it? Leeks—leaks.

I came back with: What's a drummer's favorite vegetable? Can you guess the answer? While you're thinking about it, I have another one that's similar. What's a percussionist's favorite food? Drumsticks!

In case you didn't get the drummer pun, the answer is beets (beats).

Writing time!

Write a story about one or more of these:

✦ An intelligent ant watching people at a picnic and trying to get some food.

✦ A medieval knight having a meal with you in a present-day restaurant.

✦ Something awful, but not tragic, that happened to you.

Punning time!

List a bunch of foods. Stare at the list. Look for double meanings. See if they can be shaped into favorite-food puns.

Have fun!

Save what you wrote.

CHAPTER 26

* ⋆ *

The Right Moniker

NAMES ARE important. Take the tale of Rumpelstiltskin. The whole story would fall apart if his name were Robert.

Often we meet people whose parents gave them the wrong names. The person and the name just do not match. We don't want to do that in fiction. Unless we're aiming for humor, we probably don't want to name our hero Elmer or our heroine Claribel.

So how do you find the right name?

I often use a baby-naming book for first names. The book may provide a brief history of a name and its meaning, which are sometimes helpful. Myths can suggest names. Phone books and school yearbooks can help with both first and last names.

Occasionally I take names from real life, once in a while from kids I meet when I visit schools. Some names come from my past. For example, *Dave at Night* is connected to my father's childhood, and his name was Dave. It gives me great pleasure to see his name in my book.

You can be imaginative in your name hunts. When I wrote *For Biddle's Sake*, I looked in my encyclopedia to find the name of a fairy who likes to turn people into toads. I called her Bombina, which is the scientific name of a fire-bellied toad. In *Princess Sonora and the Long Sleep* the fairy who casts the evil spell on Sonora is named Belladonna. The real belladonna is a poisonous plant.

When I use a baby-naming book or other resource, I make a list of the names I prefer. Then I choose the one that fits my character best. I picked the name Wilma for the main character in *The Wish* because it seemed perfect for an unpopular girl, and so far that has turned out to be right. But trends in names change. Twenty years ago I could have chosen Hannah instead of Wilma. Nowadays Hannah is a common name, and a Hannah can easily be popular. Years ago parents actually named their children Gail, and now most of them don't recognize a truly great name when they see it!

In addition to people, you may be naming animals and pets in your stories. You can honor your own pet by using his name, or you can try a web search on "names for pets" and find plenty of suggestions.

Since much of what I write is fantasy, I often have to

come up with names for kingdoms and towns and villages. To do it, I usually look in an atlas. First I observe the kinds of letter combinations and sounds that suggest places, like names ending in *ia* (as in Austral*ia*) or *land* (as in Eng*land*) or *io* (as in Ontar*io*). Then I mix and match and change a letter here or there. That's how I got Kyrria in *Ella Enchanted* and *Fairest* and Ontio town and Ontio castle in *Fairest*.

Your story needs a name, too. Some writers have a genius for titles. The rest of us have to work hard at it.

One approach is to think about the theme of your story. Summarize the theme in a few words, the fewer the better. Try several ways to express the theme, and write them down. Your title may be right there within the theme—a clause or a word, staring up at you.

Underline significant phrases in your story. One of them might make a satisfying title. Or your main character's name could form the title or part of the title. Lots of classic books are named after their main characters: *Peter Pan, Heidi,* and *Black Beauty*, for example.

Writing time!

Think of names for each of these characters. You can use a baby-naming book, a phone book, or anything else to help you.

- A countess who collects antique buttons
- A boy who stutters except when he's lying
- A sprite who lives in a marsh and plays a fiddle
- A peasant in France during the nineteenth century who is artistic but has little opportunity to express his talent
- A dog that loves children and that runs away from home whenever she can
- A yellow parrot that speaks seven languages
- A high school senior whose favorite subject is science, who has had the same one and only friend since kindergarten
- A small and wiry tap dancer in the 1940s who has appeared in several movies
- An eighteen-year-old loner who writes poetry and repairs motorcycles
- An underweight dragon with a weak flame

Have fun!
Save what you wrote.

* ˟ ˟

CHAPTER 27

Fiddling with Fairy Tales

FAIRY TALES ARE DEEP. Powerful. Many—"Beauty and the Beast" and "The Frog Prince," for example—are about being loved. In my opinion, "Hansel and Gretel" is about abandonment, while "Snow White" is about jealousy and "Cinderella" is about being unappreciated.

When you retell fairy tales, you tap into that depth and power. There's the richness of the magic, too: cloaks of invisibility, seven-league boots, purses that fill themselves, tablecloths that set themselves and provide food endlessly. In a fairy tale titled "The Goose Girl," there's even a dead horse's head that talks.

When fairy tales are told traditionally, the magic flashes by. You put on a cloak of invisibility, and *poof!* you're invisible. The fairy tale never says what it feels like to be invisible or whether you can see yourself or if anyone can hear you.

In fairy tales people get turned into stone, into trees, into frogs, into deer. Well, what's that like? Does the transformation hurt? If someone gets turned into a frog, does she want to eat insects, or does she still like hamburgers?

I love to imagine in full what these magical events feel like and how they work. In *For Biddle's Sake*, one of the Princess Tales, I gloried in writing about how it might feel to turn into a toad and what it might be like to be a person in a toad's body.

The neat thing about fairy tales is that you're free to imagine them any way you like. Your elf doesn't have to have pointy ears. She can have big, hairy ones or the tiniest ears imaginable, just puffs of skin around a pinprick of a hole. And your giant can be gigantic only in comparison to a mosquito.

Most fairy tales are old, so old that nobody owns them anymore. They're no longer protected by copyright, so you can play around with them. If you think Cinderella should have seven stepsisters, so be it. If you decide that the queen in "Snow White" wants to know who has the longest neck of all, go right ahead.

When I'm choosing a fairy tale to revamp, I look either for something that annoys me or for mysteries and leaps of logic.

In "The Princess and the Pea," for example, the king and queen are looking for a "true princess" for the prince, their pride and joy, to marry. So what do they come up with as a test of her princess essence?

It's a leap of logic and a mystery. What are the king and queen thinking? When the true princess becomes a queen and has life-and-death power over her subjects, will a pea-under-mattresses sensitivity help her make wise decisions?

I don't think so.

That's what got me writing *The Princess Test*, another of my Princess Tales.

Love at first sight appears in lots of fairy tales, as well as in thousands of books and movies. In fairy tales the prince usually falls for the maiden because she's pretty and sweet, and she usually falls for him because he's handsome and a prince. That's not good enough.

When I wrote *Ella Enchanted*, I had to deal with the love between the prince and Cinderella. It didn't make sense to me that they'd be so nuts about each other after dancing together a few times. That's why I made Ella and Char meet long before the balls.

There are plenty of fairy tales I haven't touched so far. But even if I have, or another author has, you can write your own version.

Writing time!

Write a story about why the prince in "Beauty and the Beast" was turned into a beast. If you've read a version or seen a movie that says why, ignore that explanation and make up your own. Be sure to describe what it feels like to turn into a beast and exactly what your beast looks like.

Next, retell the story of Rumpelstiltskin. Explain why the gnome wants the queen's baby. Then explain why he gives the queen a second chance to keep her child, by guessing his name. Solve any other mysteries you find.

Have fun!

Save what you wrote.

Writing Forever

* ⋆ *

CHAPTER 28

Writing for Your Spirit

WHEN BIG THINGS happen in my life, I write about them, either on a steno pad or on my computer. This is writing that I'll never use directly in my fiction. But the feelings and ideas I express are likely to filter, transformed and disguised, into my books.

Still, this kind of writing uses up time that I could spend on my books. So why do I do it?

I do it because I need to, because it settles me, helps me process events. When terrorists attacked the World Trade Center and the Pentagon, I didn't write about the attack for a week, not until I met with my workshop kids. I wasn't ready before that. The exercise I gave us for the day was to write a letter about the disaster to ourselves fifteen years in the future. The letter wasn't to be about the facts, because those had been recorded in newspapers and were going to be written about in books. We were to write about where we were when we found out, what we thought about, what we felt, what happened to us in our daily lives.

We usually stop after writing for twenty minutes to half an hour, but on that day we kept writing and writing. Usually I encourage everyone to share his or her work so we can make comments, but that day I said it would be fine if we didn't want to share. When we got together the next week, only one person and I were willing to read aloud. When I read mine, I skipped some parts because I sounded so cowardly and some parts because they were so sad.

The point is that what I wrote had power over me. Maybe not over anybody else. I didn't craft my words or do anything to make them dramatic.

I also record happy events. I wrote about *Ella Enchanted*'s winning the Newbery Honor, and I wrote about all the other wonderful things that happened after *Ella* was published. I wrote about when my husband stopped smoking and when I quit my job to become a full-time writer.

This writing nurtures me. I explore my feelings and feel them more deeply. I'd even go so far as to say that this writing strengthens my humanity and my understanding of others.

It also makes me more of a writer. It makes writing penetrate all the way into the marrow of my bones. It makes writing as natural for me as thinking and talking.

When you do it, save this writing, too.

Let writing be your solace, your companion, your secret joy.

Writing time!

You're going to do what we did: Write a letter to yourself fifteen years in the future. Tell yourself about the most recent big event in your life. It can be something that happened to a lot of people, or to just you. It can be something splendid or something terrible. Explain how the event happened and how you felt about it and what you did and who said what. Don't omit a single thing. Write about it till you're tearing your hair out, trying to think of one more thing to say. Then put it away in a safe place, and remember to look at it in fifteen years.

Here's another exercise, but not for today unless today is your birthday. When your birthday comes around, write about it. You don't have to make it a letter to your future self. Do it in any form you like. Write about your party if you had one, the presents you got, who gave you what, what the gifts meant to you, what you feel you accomplished in the last year, the ways you grew, what was lousy about the last year. Write about what your new age means to you. Write every single thing you can think of about your birthday, the good parts and the bad.

Do this on your next birthday and your next, forever!

Have fun, even if what you're writing about is miserable! This may be an odd kind of fun—the fun of getting it down, maybe the fun of being overdramatic. The fun of pitying yourself. You're celebrating yourself whether you're writing about misery or joy.

Save what you wrote.

CHAPTER 29

Putting Your Words Out There

THERE ARE OODLES OF books on getting published. Your public library has them. Your local bookstore has them. I have only a few things to say on the subject.

Not long ago a girl wrote to me, asking how to get one of her stories published. She said that I could look at the first three chapters of her story on the internet, and she gave me the website. As soon as she mentioned the internet, I thought, Oh, no!

Can you guess why?

Because she'd already published the story, or at least the first three chapters.

When a manuscript is accepted for publication, the publisher doesn't buy it completely or forever. The publisher buys rights to publish it in certain locations and in a certain language for a specified period.

For example, HarperCollins, an American publisher,

bought the *exclusive* right to publish *Ella Enchanted* in English in North America and the Philippines for as long as the book generated a certain amount of income every year. A while later Bertelsmann, a German publisher, bought the *exclusive* right to publish the book in German throughout the world for seven years. Listening Library bought the *exclusive* right to produce the book as an audiotape in English for twelve years.

Notice the word *exclusive*. That word is the problem for the girl who wrote to me. She can't sell the exclusive right to her story because she's made it available for free on the web. The publisher can't earn anything from it because no one's going to buy a story that's out there free for downloading.

Now, if the three chapters are the beginning of a thirty-chapter book, it doesn't matter much. She can still offer exclusive rights, and the three chapters can be considered advertising to interest readers in the whole book. But if her story has only five chapters, there's a problem.

Actually, I think it's a good idea to publish stories on the internet so long as you don't want to sell them afterward. They may find readers, and you may get helpful comments. Some sites accept everything that comes along, and some pick and choose. Some cost money, and some are free. I'm told that some even pay for the contributions they accept. You can find a variety of sites by doing a web search on "young writers."

There are also opportunities for kids to break into print on paper. Usually these come from magazines for children. Most won't pay you, and most accept only short pieces, such as poems or very short stories. But it's still a big achievement if your work is accepted. One way to find out about such opportunities is to look at a book titled *The Young Writer's Guide to Getting Published*, written by Kathy Henderson and published by Writer's Digest Books. Your library is likely to have it.

If you're submitting your writing to the kind of publisher that doesn't accept every submission, then you may experience the dreaded *REJECTION!*

Some publishers will accept entire manuscripts only from literary agents. Some of these publishers, however, will accept a descriptive letter, called a query letter, and sample chapters from unknown writers.

Those publishers that accept complete manuscripts receive lots and lots and lots (and throw in as many more *lots* as you can imagine) of submissions, more than their editors can go through quickly. When a manuscript reaches a publisher, it goes to the bottom of a stack of other manuscripts. That stack has a name, a terrible name, the slush pile. It can take ten months or more for a manuscript to reach the top of the pile. It's lucky you're starting young!

There's more bad news. Each manuscript is competing

against every other submission, and the publisher can accept only a few.

Almost every author I know has gotten rejections. I may be the queen of rejection letters. During my long trek toward being published, my stories, mostly picture books, were turned down by every children's book publisher I could find. Most of the rejections were form letters, which I threw away. If I hadn't, I could have wallpapered my house with them.

I did save the personal rejection letters, and the folder that holds them is two inches thick. The worst one said that my plots were rotten, and my stories had no emotional depth and no character development. When I visit schools, I take this letter with me and read it to kids.

Why do I do that? Isn't it embarrassing?

It's not embarrassing. We all get rejections. In fact I've heard of a writers' group in which the members compete to see who'll receive the most rejection letters in a year, and the winner gets a prize.

Yes, a prize! Because the person who gets the most rejection letters will, in the end, get the most acceptance phone calls. She's put herself out there. She's learning from the editorial responses. She's writing away. She's believing in herself.

The terrible rejection letter that made me miserable when I got it no longer has any power to hurt me. It's a treasured possession now, proof of how far I've come.

Surprisingly, sometimes rejection can be your friend. *Dave at Night* was rejected umpty-ump times and revised umpty-ump times plus one, which did the trick. After it finally came out, I was signing copies of it at a conference when an editor asked me to sign hers. She was one of the editors who had rejected the manuscript years before, and she told me that she had loved it then and had wanted to accept it. But other people at the publisher where she worked hadn't liked it, so she hadn't been able to.

I'd had no idea she liked the book. At the time I would have sold my teeth to have gotten *Dave* or anything else published. But as she walked away, my only thought was: Thank heavens she didn't accept it. Because the book that was published, the one I like to think you've read, is a much better book.

Was final success worth all the rejection? Yes! A thousand times yes. Because kids are reading my stories. My words and my ideas are entering their minds, maybe making them see the world in a new way, maybe becoming part of them. What could be better?

Writing time!

Write two stories based on one of the choices below, one that ends happily and one that doesn't. Keep in mind that each version is a different story. If they're both the same except for the ending, the stories will seem forced.

+ Lori asks James to be her date to the school graduation party.
+ Baxter is working on a news story to submit to the local newspaper.
+ Allie is trying out for the soccer team.

Now, if you like, write two stories each based on the options above that you didn't choose.

Have fun!

Save what you wrote.

✦ ✶ ✦

CHAPTER 30

Exeunt Writing

WE BEGAN WITH writing. Let's end the same way.

Writing time!

Before you do this exercise, turn to the contents page or to the index and run your eyes down the topics. Now try to put everything into the exercise: detail and method writing and suffering for your characters and readers and not much self-criticism for you.

In Chapter 5, "Getting into It," I used a story idea about a bank robbery as an example. We're going back to the bank.

Annie is there with her cousin and her aunt when the robbery happens. Pick one of the following options about Annie, or blend a few of them together.

- Annie has a black belt in karate. She wants to be a police officer or a firefighter when she grows up.
- Annie has been studying tae kwan do for three

months. She's not good at it, but she doesn't know that, and she's overly self-confident.

+ Annie's father was attacked on the street two weeks ago. He was shot and is in the hospital. The doctors aren't sure he'll live.

+ Annie recognizes the robber as her best friend's older brother.

+ Annie is blind.

+ Annie is so wrapped up in telling her cousin something that she doesn't realize a robbery is going on.

+ Annie is telepathic. She can read the robber's mind.

Do not read ahead!

Do not turn the page!

Write at least three pages or a whole story.
Now turn the page, and read on.

Here are some options about the robber. Pick one or blend a few together:

+ This is Brent's first robbery.
+ Brent's gun isn't real.
+ Brent hates children and teenagers.
+ Annie looks a lot like Brent's own daughter.
+ Brent has memorized what he has to say to the teller, but he doesn't speak or understand English.
+ Brent's mother is the manager of the bank.
+ Brent is in a wheelchair.

Don't change Annie. Revise your story or write a new story incorporating the options you chose for Brent.

Have fun!

Save what you wrote.

Here are my parting words: I had the best time writing this book. I hope you've had a great time reading it and trying out the exercises. I hope writing has become part of you. I hope you have much much much success with your stories. I'd like to hear about your achievements. Write to me at my publisher and tell me. I may not have time to answer your letters, but I'll read them, and I'll know, and I'll be in your corner, rooting for you.

Write to nurture yourself.

Write to tell us about being you.

Write to tell us about being human.

There can never be too many stories. Add to the reservoir.

Save every word.
Have fun!

Index